Piano • Vocal • Gui

The

BIG BOOK
OF HYMNS

ISBN 0-634-00699-1

HAL•LEONARD®
CORPORATION
7777 W. BLUEMOUND RD. P.O. BOX 13819 MILWAUKEE, WI 53213

Visit Hal Leonard Online at
www.halleonard.com

CONTENTS

ABIDE WITH ME

Words by HENRY F. LYTE
Music by W.H. MONK

Moderately Slow

A - bide with me. Fast falls the e - ven - tide.
I need Thy pre - sence ev - 'ry pass - ing hour.

The dark - ness deep - ens, Lord, with me a - bide.
What but thy grace can foil the tempt - er's pow'r?

When oth - er help - ers fail and com - forts flee,
Who, like Thy - self, my guide and stay can be?

Help of the
Through cloud and

ALL CREATURES OF OUR GOD AND KING

Words by FRANCIS OF ASSISI
Music from *Geistliche Kirchengesäng*

ALL GLORY, LAUD AND HONOR

Text by THEODULPH OF ORLEANS
Translation by JOHN M. NEALE
Music by MELCHIOR TESCHNER

With dignity

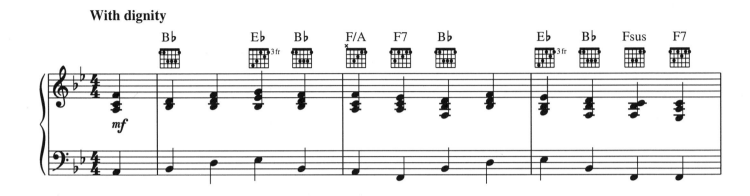

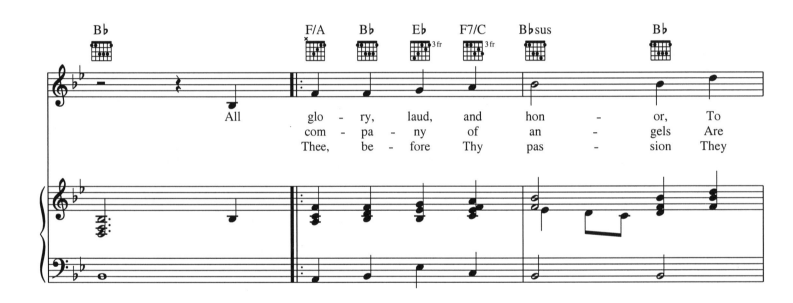

All glo - ry, laud, and hon - or, To
com - pa - ny of an - gels Are
Thee, be - fore Thy pas - sion They

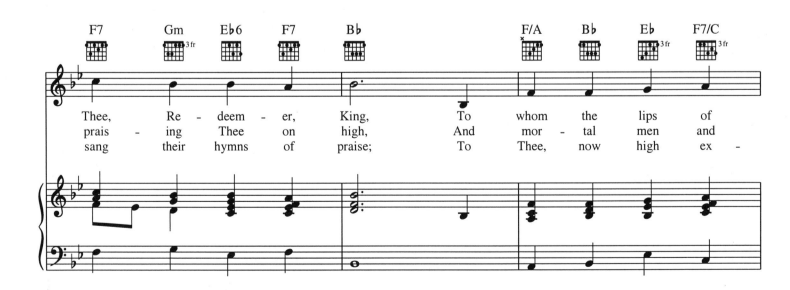

Thee, Re - deem - er, King, To whom the lips of
prais - ing Thee on high, And mor - tal men and
sang their hymns of praise; To Thee, now high ex -

ALL HAIL THE POWER OF JESUS' NAME

Words by EDWARD PERRONET (v. 1,3)
Words by JOHN RIPPON (v. 2,4)
Music by OLIVER HOLDEN

All hail the power of Je - sus' name. Let an - gels pros - trate

fall. Bring forth the roy - al di - a - dem and

2. Let ev'ry kindred, ev'ry tribe on this terrestrial ball.
   To Him all majesty ascribe and crown Him Lord of all.
   To Him all majesty ascribe and crown Him Lord of all.

3. Oh, that with yonder sacred throng we at his feet may fall.
   We'll join the everlasting song and crown Him Lord of all.
   We'll join the everlasting song and crown Him Lord of all.

ALL THE WAY MY SAVIOR LEADS ME

Words by FANNY J. CROSBY
Music by ROBERT LOWRY

ALL THINGS BRIGHT AND BEAUTIFUL

Words by CECIL FRANCES ALEXANDER
17th Century English Melody
Arranged by MARTIN SHAW

AM I A SOLDIER OF THE CROSS

Words by ISAAC WATTS
Music by THOMAS A. ARNE

AMAZING GRACE

Words by JOHN NEWTON
Traditional American Melody

Verse 3
And when this flesh and heart shall fail
and mortal life shall cease.
I shall possess within the veil
a life of joy and peace.

When we've been there ten thousand years,
bright shining as the sun.

We've no less days to sing God's praise
than when we first begun.

ASK YE WHAT GREAT THING I KNOW

Words by JOHANN C. SCHWEDLER
Music by H.A. CÉSAR MALAN

COME, THOU ALMIGHTY KING

Anonymous Text
Music by FELICE DE GIARDINI

With An Easy Flow

3. Come, holy Comforter!
   Thy sacred witness bear,
   In this glad hour:
   Thou who almighty art,
   Now rule in ev'ry heart,
   And ne'er from us depart,
   Spirit of pow'r!

4. To the great One in Three,
   The highest praises be,
   Hence ever more!
   His sov'reign majesty
   May we in glory see,
   And to eternity
   Love and adore.

BATTLE HYMN OF THE REPUBLIC

Words by JULIA WARD HOWE
Music by WILLIAM STEFFE

1. Mine eyes have seen the glo - ry of the com - ing of the Lord. He is
2. seen him in the watch-fires of the hun - dred cir - cling camps. They have
3.-5. *(See additional verses)*

tramp - ling out the vin - tage where the grapes of wrath are stored. He hath
build - ed Him an al - tar in the eve - ning dews and damps. I have

loos'd the fate - ful light - ning of His ter - ri - ble swift sword. His
read His right - eous sen - tence by the dim and flar - ing lamps. His

Additional Verses

3. I have read a fiery gospel writ in burnished rows of steel.
   As ye deal with my contempters, so with you my grace shall deal.
   Let the hero born of woman crush the serpent with his heel,
   Since God is marching on.

4. He has sounded forth the trumpet that shall never call retreat
   He is sifting out the hearts of men before His judgement seat.
   O be swift, my soul, to answer Him, be jubilant, my feet.
   Our God is marching on.

5. In the beauty of the lilies, Christ was born across the sea.
   With a glory in His bosom that transfigures you and me.
   As He died to make men holy, let us die to make men free,
   While God is marching on.

BE THOU MY VISION

Traditional Irish

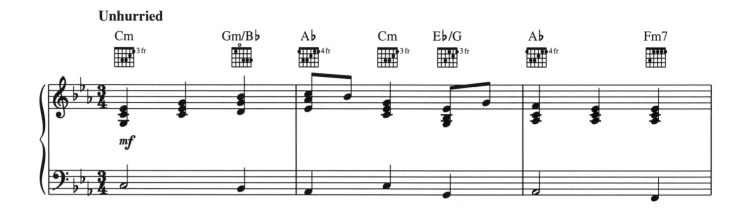

Be thou my _____ vi - sion, O
Be thou my _____ wis - dom, and
Great God of _____ heav - en, my

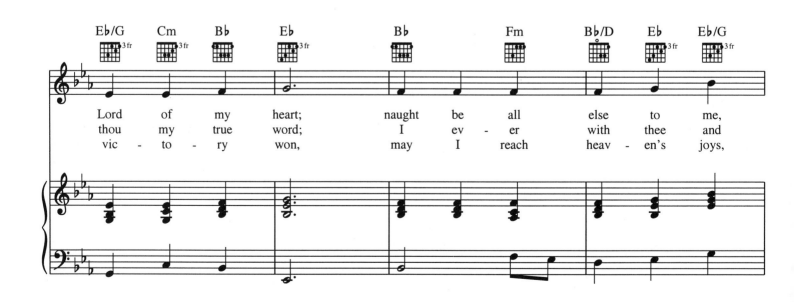

Lord of my heart; naught be all else to me.
thou my true word; I ev - er with thee and
vic - to - ry won, may I reach heav - en's joys,

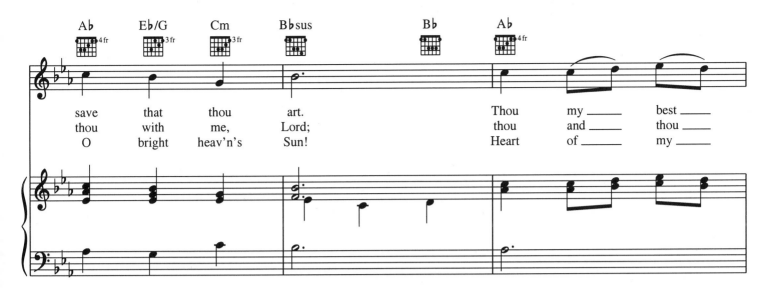

save that thou art. Thou my best
thou with me, Lord; thou and thou
O bright heav'n's Sun! Heart of my

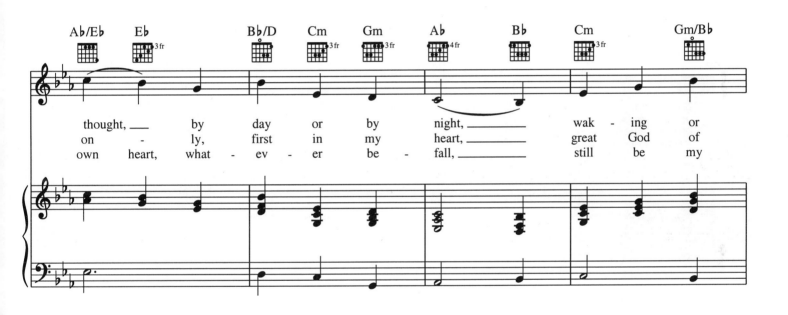

thought, by day or by night, wak - ing or
on - ly, first in my heart, great God of
own heart, what - ev - er be - fall, still be my

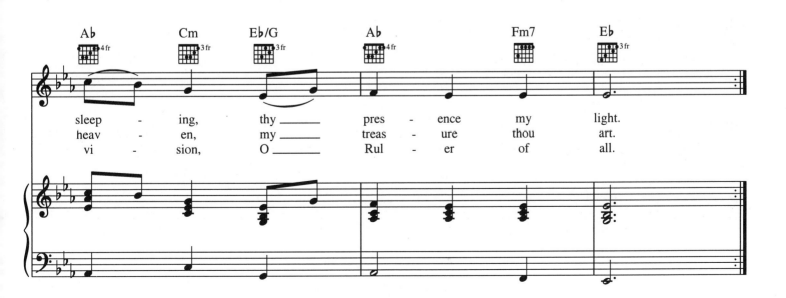

sleep - ing, thy pres - ence my light.
heav - en, my treas - ure thou art.
vi - sion, O Rul - er of all.

BEAUTIFUL ISLE OF SOMEWHERE

Words by JESSIE BROWN POUNDS
Music by JOHN S. FEARIS

BENEATH THE CROSS OF JESUS

Words by ELIZABETH C. CLEPHANE
Music by FREDERICK C. MAKER

BLESSED ASSURANCE

Lyrics by FANNY CROSBY and VAN ALSTYNE
Music by PHOEBE P. KNAPP

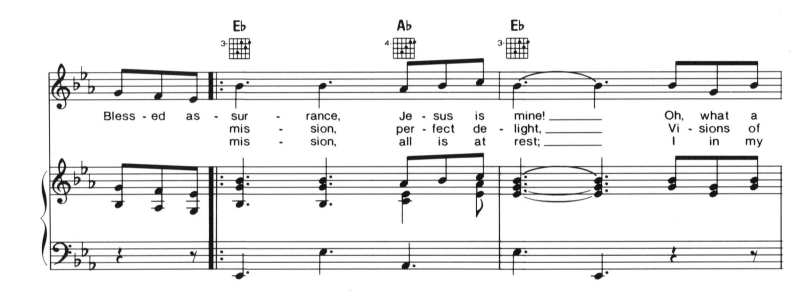

Bless-ed as - sur - rance, Je - sus is mine! _____ Oh, what a
mis - sion, per - fect de - light, _____ Vi - sions of
mis - sion, all is at rest; _____ I in my

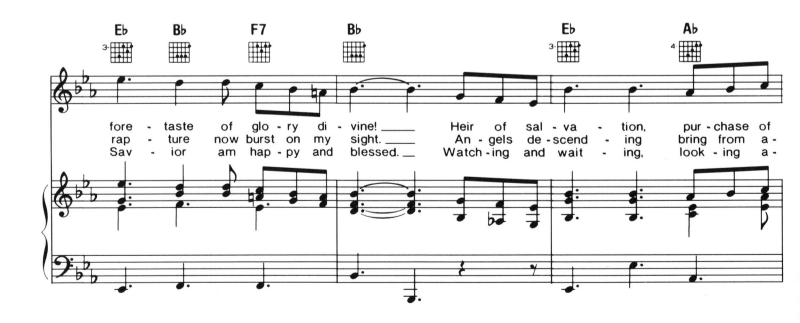

fore - taste of glo - ry di - vine! _____ Heir of sal - va - tion, pur - chase of
rap - ture now burst on my sight. _____ An - gels de - scend - ing bring from a -
Sav - ior am hap - py and blessed. _ Watch - ing and wait - ing, look - ing a -

BLEST BE THE TIE THAT BINDS

Words by JOHN FAWCETT
Music by JOHANN G. NÄGELI

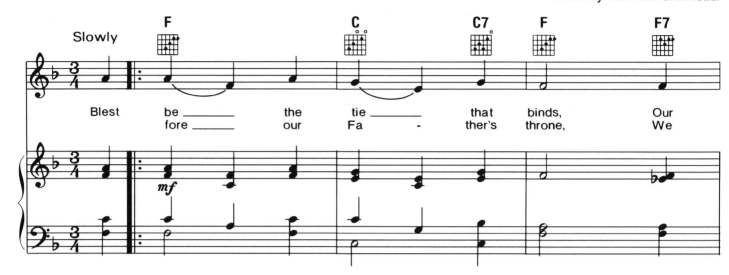

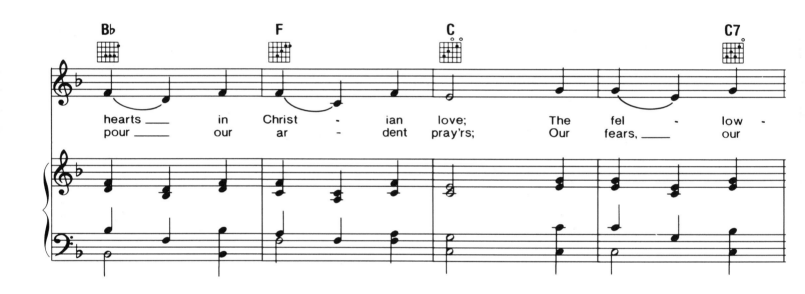

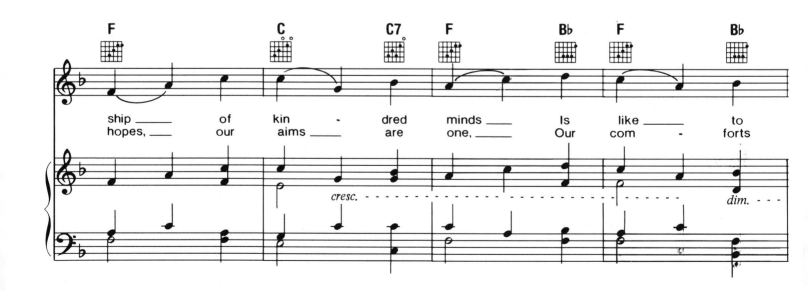

BREAK THOU THE BREAD OF LIFE

Words by MARY ARTEMESIA LATHBURY
Music by WILLIAM FISKE SHERWIN

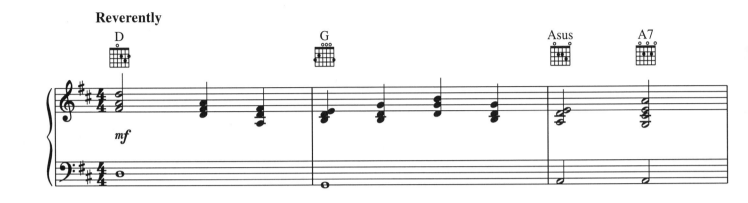

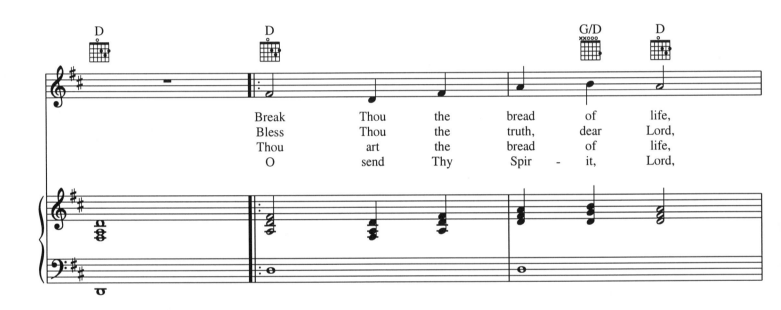

Break Thou the bread of life,
Bless Thou the truth, dear Lord,
Thou art the bread of life,
O send Thy Spir - it, Lord,

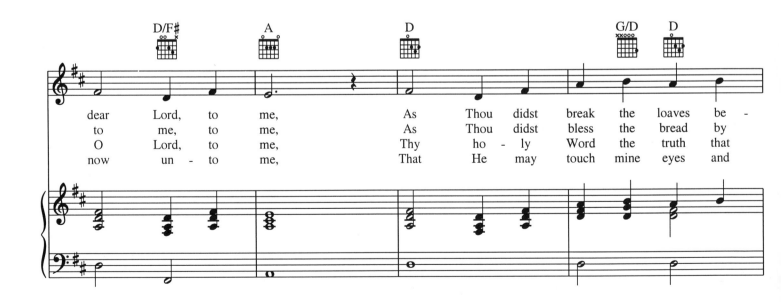

dear Lord, to me,
to me, to me,
O Lord, to me,
now un - to me,

As Thou didst break the loaves be -
As Thou didst bless the bread by
Thy ho - ly Word the truth that
That He may touch mine eyes and

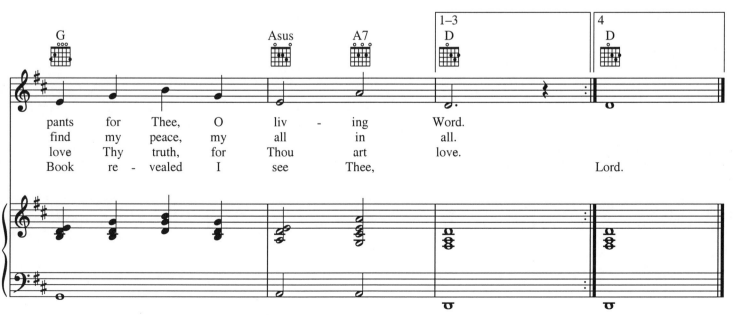

BREATHE ON ME, BREATH OF GOD

Words by EDWIN HATCH
Music by ROBERT JACKSON

BRINGING IN THE SHEAVES

Words by KNOWLES SHAW
Music by GEORGE A. MINOR

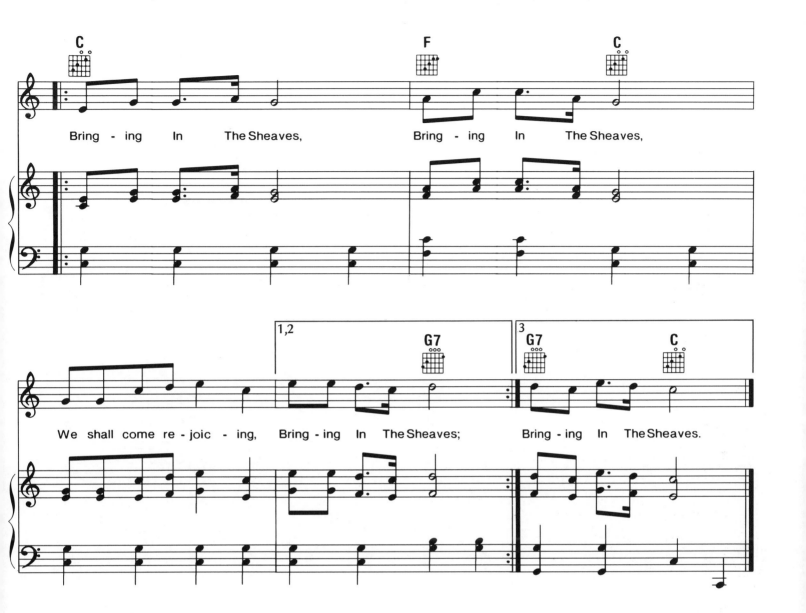

3. Going forth with weeping, sowing for the Master.
   Tho' the loss sustained our spirit often grieves;
   When our weeping's over, He will bid us welcome,
   We shall come rejoicing, bringing in the sheaves.

CHRIST THE LORD IS RISEN TODAY

Words by CHARLES WESLEY
Music adapted from *Lyra Davidica*

43

2. Lives again our glorious King: Alleluia!
   Where, O death, is now thy sting? Alleluia!
   Dying once, He all doth save: Alleluia!
   Where thy victory, O grave? Alleluia!

3. Love's redeeming work is done, Alleluia!
   Fought the fight, the battle won: Alleluia!
   Death in vain forbids Him rise: Alleluia!
   Christ has opened Paradise. Alleluia!

4. Soar we now, where Christ has led, Alleluia!
   Foll'wing our exalted Head: Alleluia!
   Made like Him, like Him we rise: Alleluia!
   Ours the cross, the grave, the skies. Alleluia!

THE CHURCH'S ONE FOUNDATION

Words by SAMUEL STONE
Music by SAMUEL WESLEY

2. Elect from every nation,
   Yet one o'er all the earth,
   Her charter of salvation,
   One Lord, one faith, one birth;
   One holy name she blesses,
   Partakes one holy food,
   And to one hope she presses,
   With every grace endued.

3. 'Mid toil and tribulation,
   And tumult of her war,
   She waits the consummation
   Of peace for evermore;
   Till with the vision glorious,
   Her longing eyes are blest,
   And the great Church victorious
   Shall be the Church at rest.

4. Yet she on earth hath union
   With God, the Three in One,
   And mystic sweet communion
   With those whose rest is won;
   O happy ones and holy!
   Lord give us grace that we
   Like them, the meek and lowly,
   On high may dwell with Thee.

CLOSE TO THEE

Words by FANNY J. CROSBY
Music by SILAS J. VAIL

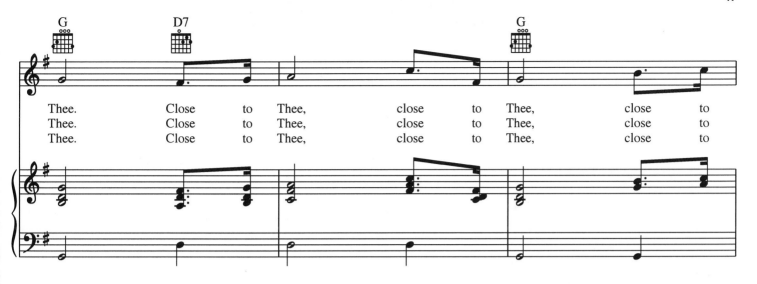

Thee. Close to Thee, close to Thee, close to
Thee. Close to Thee, close to Thee, close to
Thee. Close to Thee, close to Thee, close to

Thee, close to Thee, all a - long my pil - grim
Thee, close to Thee, glad - ly will I toil and
Thee, close to Thee, then the gate of life e -

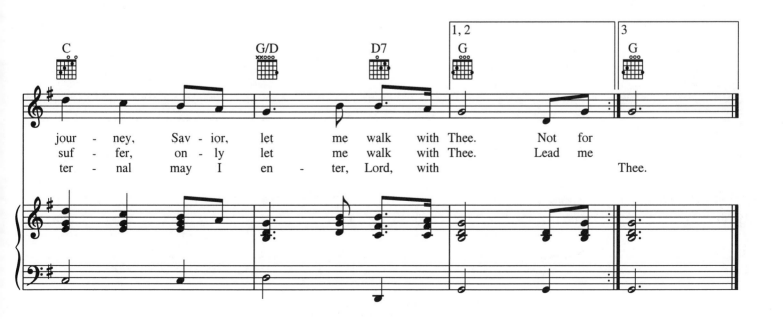

jour - ney, Sav - ior, let me walk with Thee. Not for
suf - fer, on - ly let me walk with Thee. Lead me
ter - nal may I en - ter, Lord, with Thee.

COME, THOU FOUNT OF EVERY BLESSING

Words by ROBERT ROBINSON
Traditional Music compiled by JOHN WYETH

CROWN HIM WITH MANY CROWNS

Words by MATTHEW BRIDGES and GODFREY THRING
Music by GEORGE JOB ELVEY

Crown Him with ma - ny crowns, The Lamb up - on His
Crown Him the Lord of Love! Be - hold His hands and

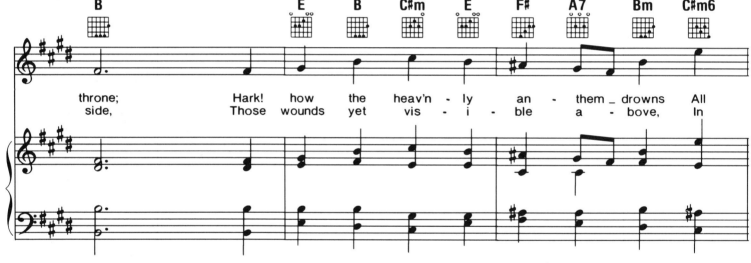

throne; Hark! how the heav'n - ly an - them _ drowns, All
side, Those wounds yet vis - i - ble a - bove, In

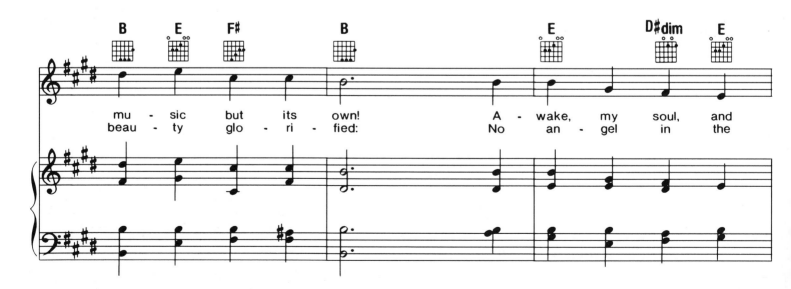

mu - sic but its own! A - wake, my soul, and
beau - ty glo - ri - fied: No an - gel in the

51

3. Crown Him the Lord of life, Who triumphed o'er the grave
And rose victorious in the strife for those He came to save.
His glories now we sing, Who dies and rose on high,
Who dies eternal life to bring and lives that death may die.

HAVE THINE OWN WAY, LORD

Words by ADELAIDE POLLARD
Music by GEORGE STEBBINS

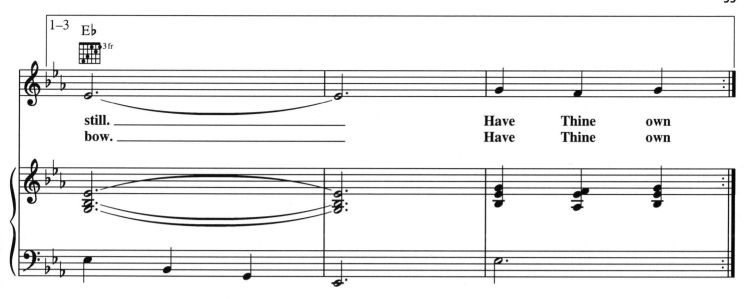

still. _____ Have Thine own
bow. _____ Have Thine own

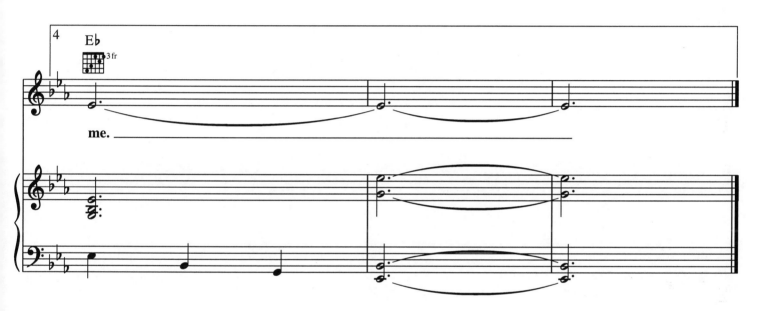

me. _____

Additional Verses

3. **Have Thine own way, Lord!**
   Have Thine own way!
   Wounded and weary, Help me, I pray!
   Power, all power
   Surely is Thine!
   Touch me and heal me, Savior divine.

4. **Have Thine own way, Lord!**
   Have Thine own way!
   Hold o'er my being Absolute sway!
   Fill with Thy Spirit
   Till all shall see
   Christ only, always, Living in me.

ETERNAL FATHER, STRONG TO SAVE

Words by W. WHITING
Music by J.B. DYKES

hear   us   when   we   cry   to   Thee   for   those   in   per - il

on   the   sea.   O   land   and   sea.   A - men.

rit.

Additional Verses

2. O Savior, whose almighty word
   The winds and waves submissive heard,
   Who walkedst on the foaming deep
   And calm amid its rage didst sleep:
   O hear us when we cry to Thee
   For those in peril on the sea.

3. O sacred Spirit, who didst brood
   Upon the chaos dark and rude,
   Who bad'st its angry tumult cease,
   And gavest light and life and peace:
   O hear us when we cry to Thee
   For those in peril on the sea.

4. O Trinity of love and power,
   Our brethren shield in danger's hour;
   From rock and tempest, fire and foe,
   Protect them wheresoe'er they go;
   And ever let there rise to Thee
   Glad hymns of praise from land and sea. Amen.

FAIREST LORD JESUS

Words for stanza 4 by JOSEPH AUGUST SEISS
Music from *Schlesische Volkslieder*
Arranged by RICHARD STORRS WILLIS

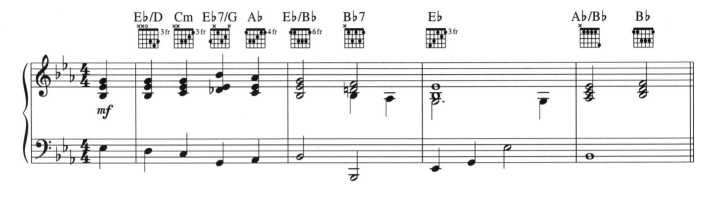

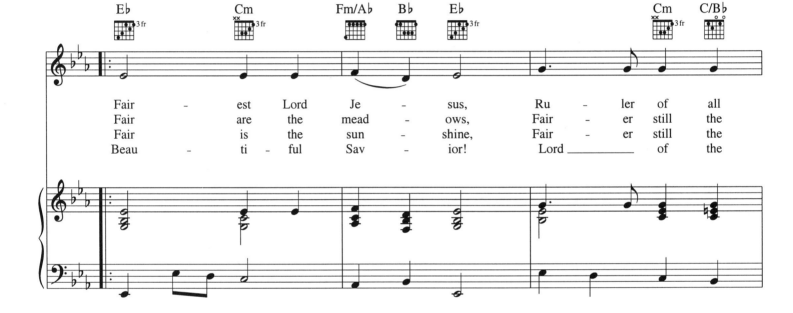

Fair - est Lord Je - sus, Ru - ler of all
Fair are the mead - ows, Fair - er still the
Fair is the sun - shine, Fair - er still the
Beau - ti - ful Sav - ior! Lord _____ of the

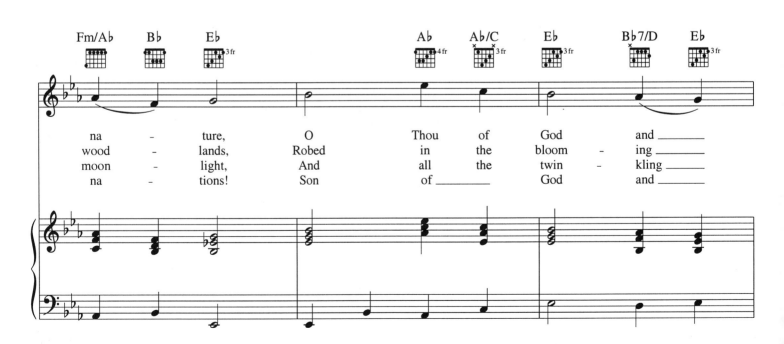

na - ture, O Thou of God and _____
wood - lands, Robed in the bloom - ing _____
moon - light, And all the twin - kling _____
na - tions! Son of _____ God and _____

FAITH OF OUR FATHERS

Words by FREDERICK W. FABER
Music by HENRI F. HEMY and JAMES G. WALTON

Faith of our fa - thers, liv - ing still
Faith of our fa - thers, we _____ will strive
Faith of our fa - thers, we _____ will love

In spite of dun - geon, fire _____ and sword;
To win all na - tions un - to thee;
Both friend and foe in all _____ our strife;

FOR ALL THE BLESSINGS OF THE YEAR

Words by ALBERT H. HUTCHINSON
Music by ROBERT N. QUAILE

For all the bless - ings of the year,
For life and health, those com - mon things,
For love of Thine, which nev - er tires,

For all the friends we hold so dear,
Which ev - 'ry day and hour brings,
Which all our bet - ter thought in - spires

FOR THE BEAUTY OF THE EARTH

Text by FOLLIOT S. PIERPOINT
Music by CONRAD KOCHER

* for Holy Communion

GOD OF OUR FATHERS

Words by DANIEL C. ROBERTS
Music by GEORGE WILLIAM WARREN

GOD WILL TAKE CARE OF YOU

Words by CIVILLA D. MARTIN
Music by W. STILLMAN MARTIN

Be not dis - mayed ___ what - e'er be - tide;
Through days of toil ___ when heart doth fail;
All you may need ___ He will pro - vide;
No mat - ter what ___ may be the test,

God will take care of you. ___

Be - neath His wings ___ of
When dan - gers fierce ___ your
Noth - ing you ask ___ will
Lean, wea - ry one, ___ up -

GUIDE ME, O THOU GREAT JEHOVAH

Words by WILLIAM WILLIAMS
Music by JOHN HUGHES

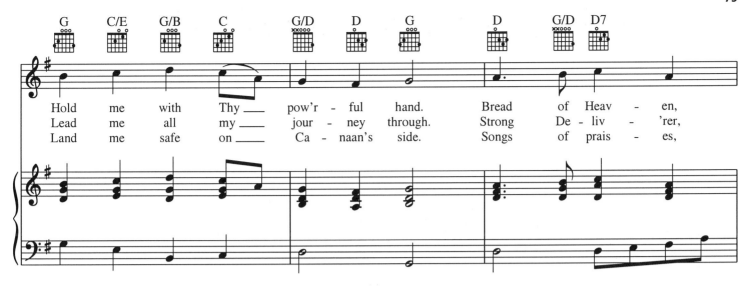

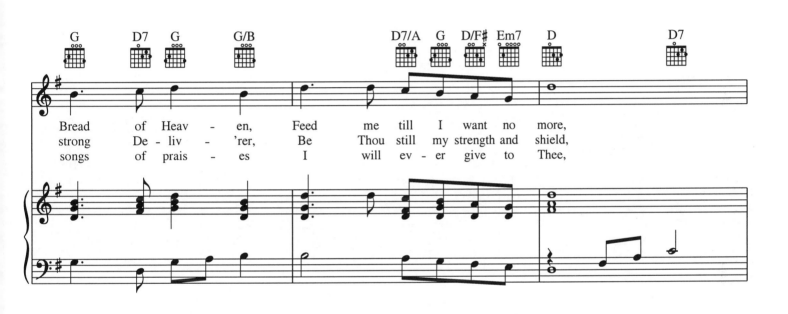

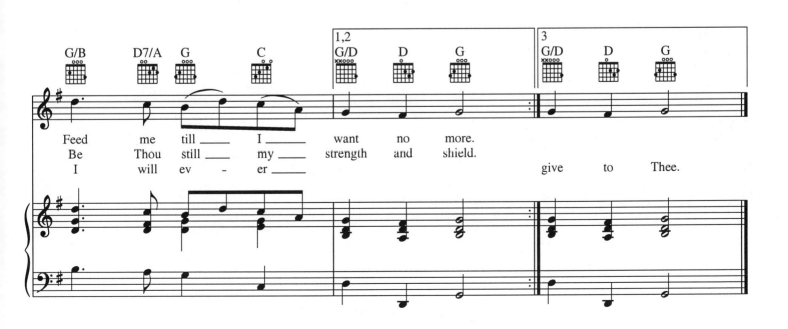

HE HIDETH MY SOUL

Words by FANNY J. CROSBY
Music by WILLIAM J. KIRKPATRICK

HE LEADETH ME

Words by JOSEPH H. GILMORE
Music by WILLIAM B. BRADBURY

HIS EYE IS ON THE SPARROW

Text by C.D. MARTIN
Music by CHARLES H. GABRIEL

HOLY, HOLY, HOLY

Text by REGINALD HEBER
Music by JOHN B. DYKES

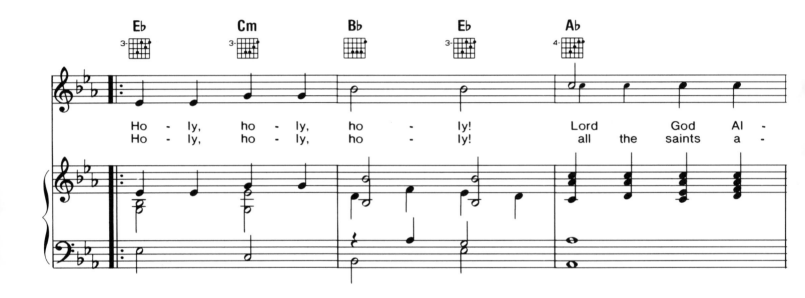

Ho - ly, ho - ly, ho - ly! Lord God Al -
Ho - ly, ho - ly, ho - ly! all the saints a -

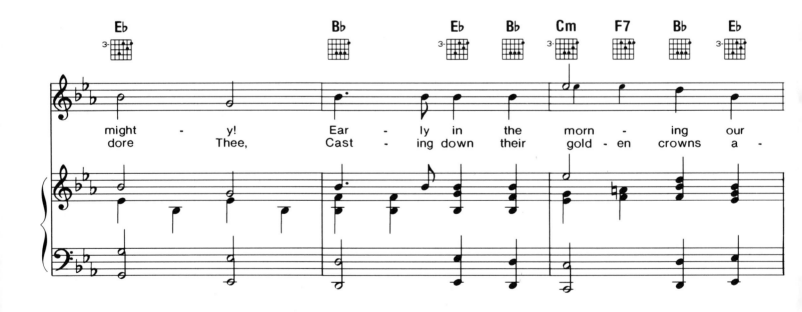

might - y! Ear - ly in the morn - ing our
dore Thee, Cast - ing down their gold - en crowns a -

I MUST TELL JESUS

Words and Music by
E.A. HOFFMAN

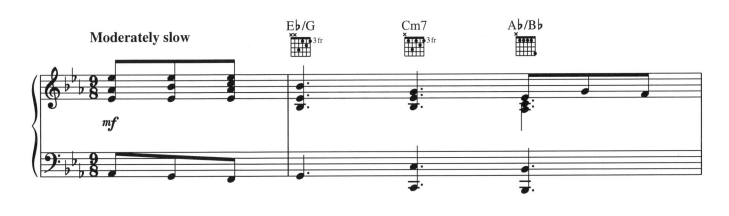

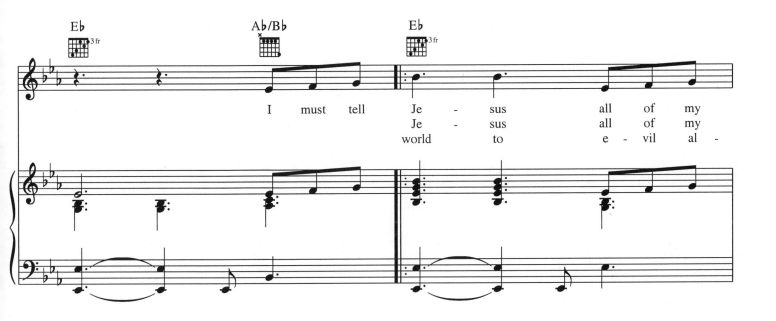

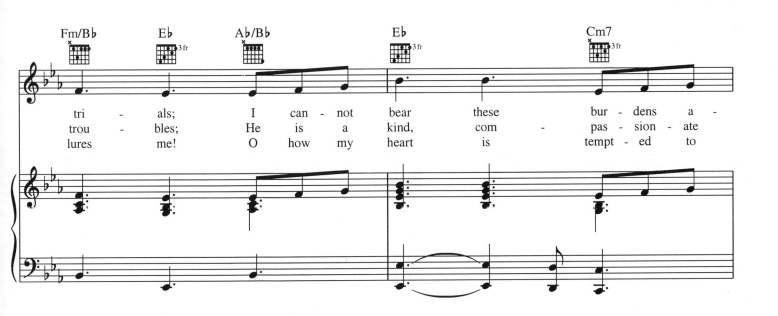

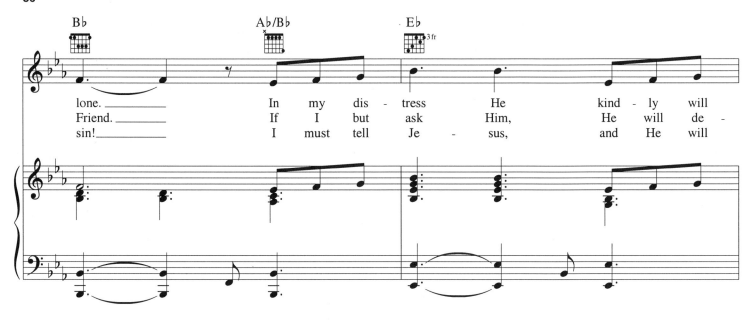

lone. _____ In my dis-tress. He kind-ly will
Friend. _____ If I but ask Him, He will de-
sin!_____ I must tell Je - sus, and He will

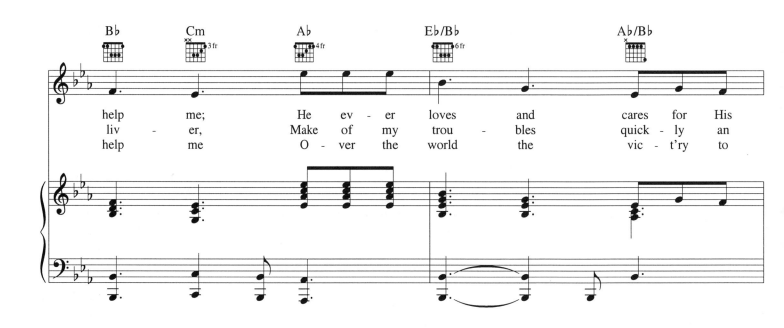

help me; He ev - er loves and cares for His
liv - er, Make of my trou-bles quick - ly an
help me O - ver the world the vic - t'ry to

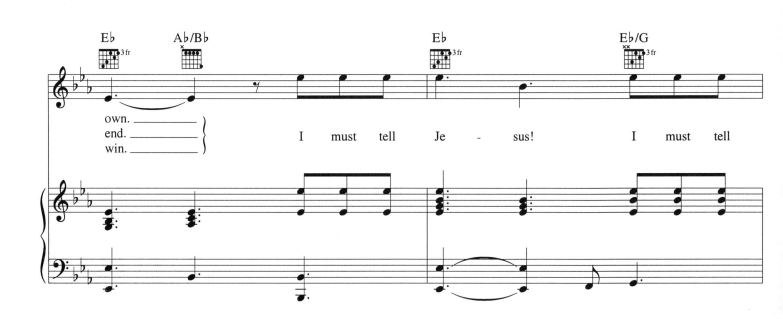

own. _____ I must tell Je - sus! I must tell
end. _____
win. _____

HOW FIRM A FOUNDATION

Traditional text compiled by JOHN RIPPON
Traditional music compiled by JOSEPH FUNK

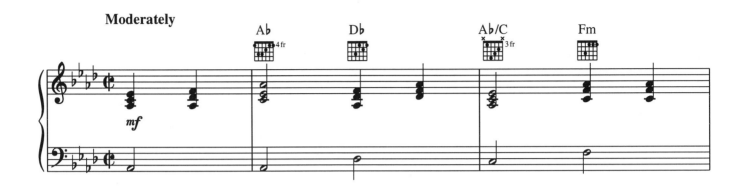

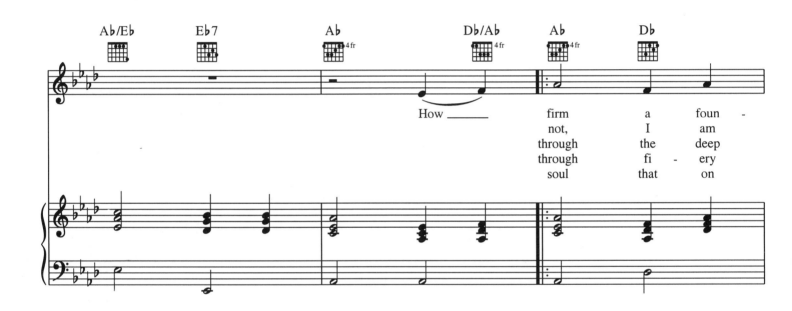

How ____ firm a foun -
not, I am
through the deep
through fi - ery
soul that on

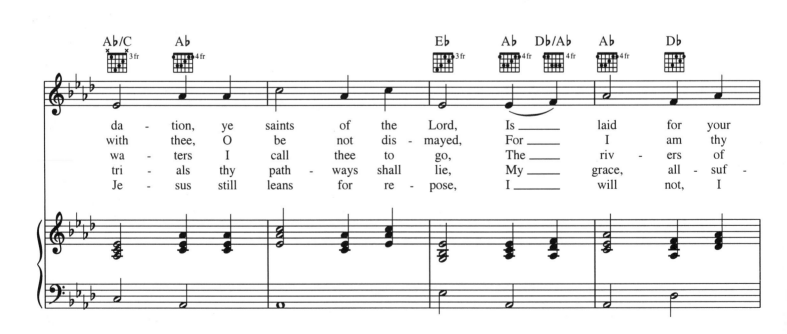

da - tion, ye saints of the Lord, Is ____ laid for your
with thee, O be not dis - mayed, For ____ I am thy
wa - ters I call thee to go, The ____ riv - ers of
tri - als thy path - ways shall lie, My ____ grace, all - suf -
Je - sus still leans for re - pose, I ____ will not, I

HOW SWEET THE NAME OF JESUS SOUNDS

Words by JOHN NEWTON
Music by ALEXANDER REINAGLE

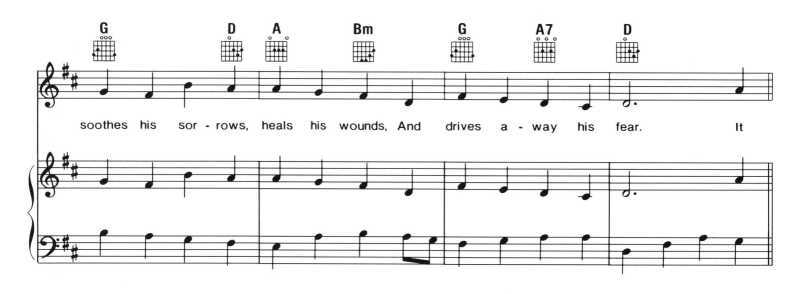

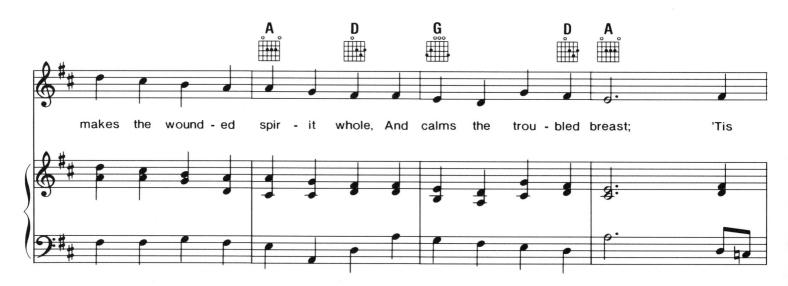

I AM THINE, O LORD

Words by FANNY J. CROSBY
Music by WILLIAM H. DOANE

I HAVE DECIDED TO FOLLOW JESUS

Words by an Indian Prince
Music by AUILA READ

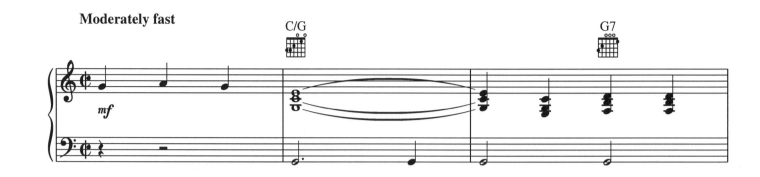

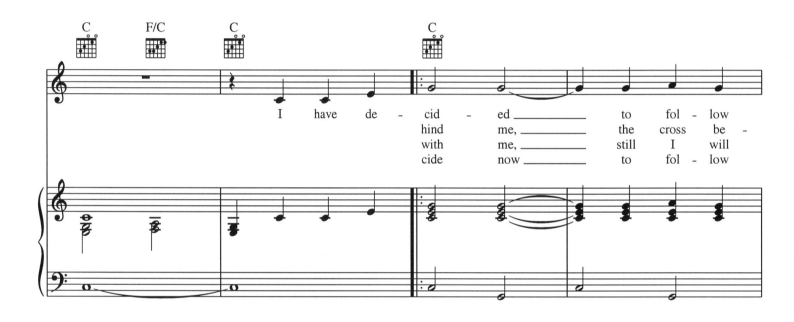

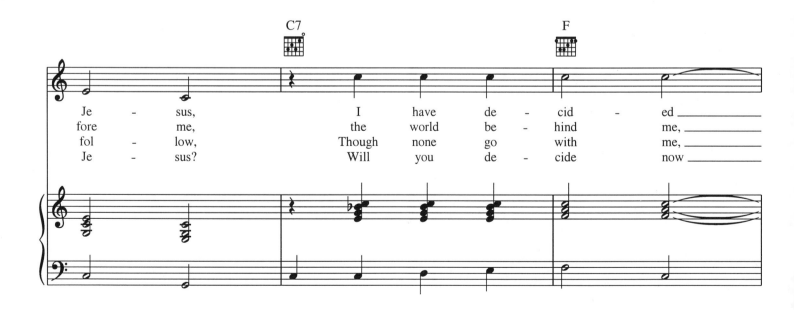

I LOVE THY KINGDOM, LORD

Words by TIM DWIGHT
Music by AARON WILLIAMS

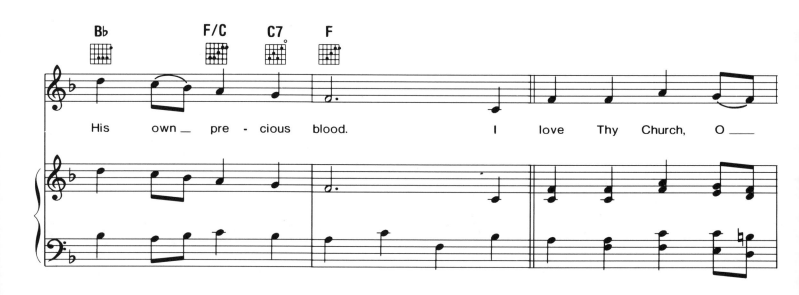

I LOVE TO TELL THE STORY

Words by A. CATHERINE HANKEY
Music by WILLIAM G. FISCHER

I NEED THEE EVERY HOUR

Words by ANNIE S. HAWKS
Music by ROBERT LOWRY

I SURRENDER ALL

Words by J.W. VAN DEVENTER
Music by W.S. WEEDEN

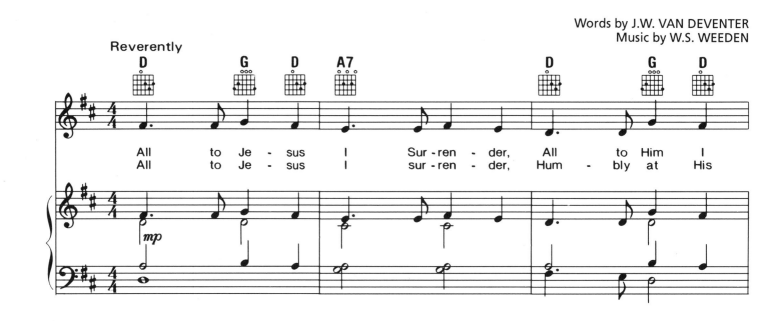

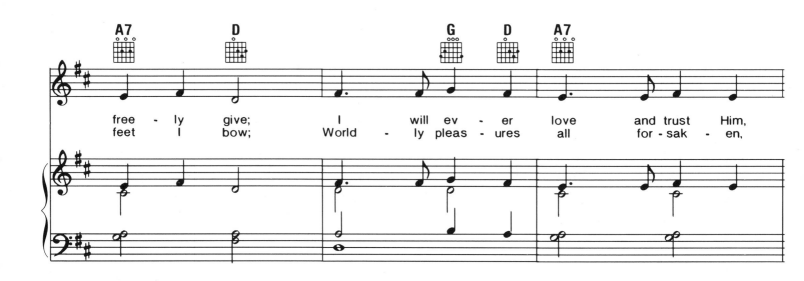

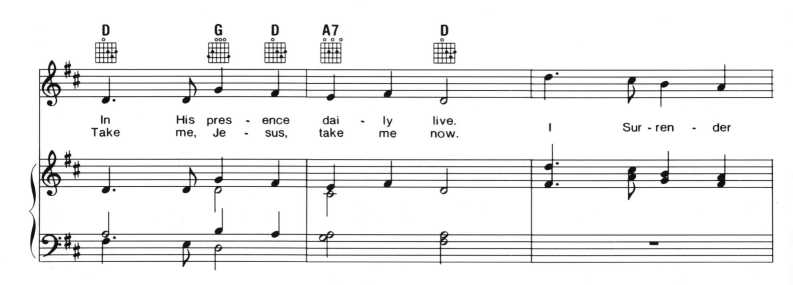

JESUS, THE VERY THOUGHT OF THEE

Words attributed to BERNARD OF CLAIRVAUX
Music by JOHN BACCHUS DYKES

I WILL SING THE WONDROUS STORY

Words by FRANCIS H. ROWLEY
Music by PETER P. BILHORN

I WOULD BE TRUE

Words by HOWARD A. WALTER
Music by JOSEPH Y. PEEK

IMMORTAL, INVISIBLE

Words by WALTER CHALMERS SMITH
Traditional Music

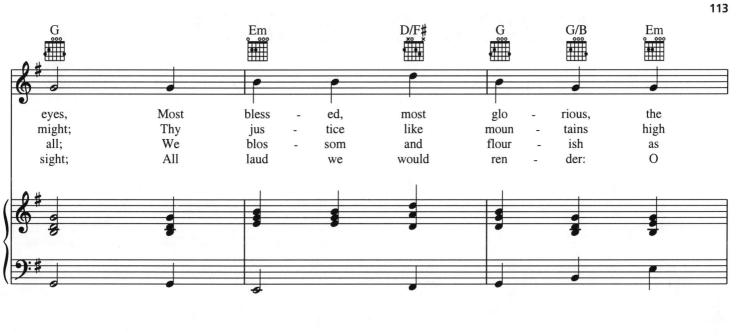

eyes, Most bless - ed, most glo - rious, the
might; Thy jus - tice like moun - tains high
all; We blos - som and flour - ish as
sight; All laud we would ren - der: O

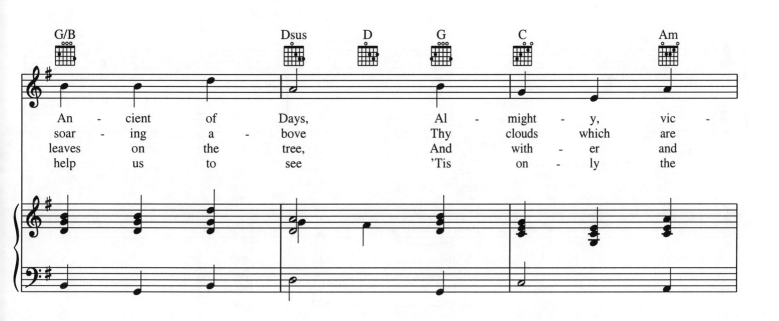

An - cient of Days, Al - might - y, vic -
soar - ing a - bove Thy clouds which are
leaves on the tree, And with - er and
help us to see 'Tis on - ly the

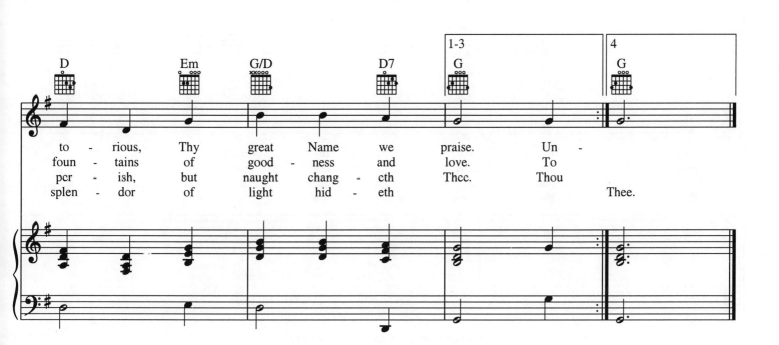

to - rious, Thy great Name we praise. Un -
foun - tains of good - ness and love. To
per - ish, but naught chang - eth Thee. Thou
splen - dor of light hid - eth Thee.

IN THE CROSS OF CHRIST I GLORY

Words by JOHN BOWRING
Music by ITHAMAR CONKEY

115

IN THE GARDEN

Words and Music by
C. AUSTIN MILES

IT IS WELL WITH MY SOUL

Text by HORATIO G. SPAFFORD
Music by PHILIP P. BLISS

JESUS IS ALL THE WORLD TO ME

Words and Music by
WILL L. THOMPSON

JESUS IS TENDERLY CALLING

Words by FANNY J. CROSBY
Music by GEORGE C. STEBBINS

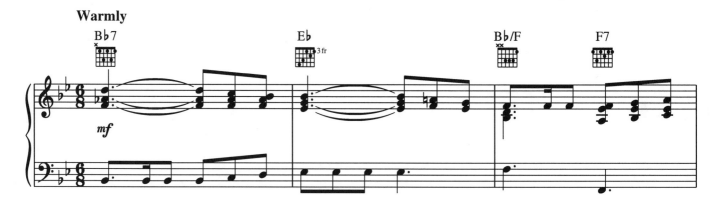

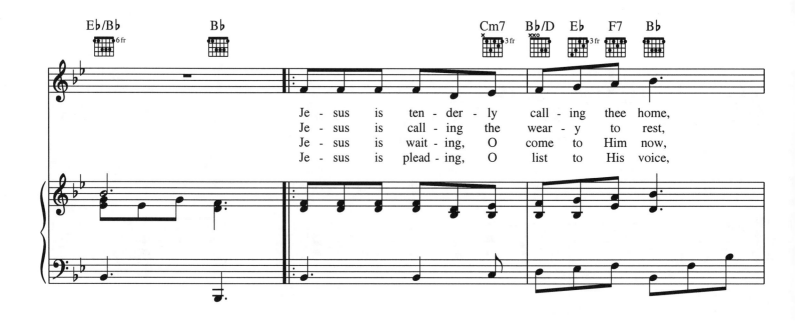

Je - sus is ten - der - ly call - ing thee home,
Je - sus is call - ing the wear - y to rest,
Je - sus is wait - ing, O come to Him now,
Je - sus is plead - ing, O list to His voice,

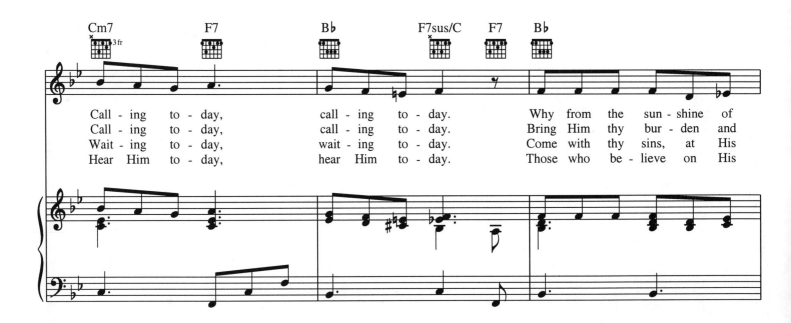

Call - ing to - day, call - ing to - day.
Call - ing to - day, call - ing to - day.
Wait - ing to - day, wait - ing to - day.
Hear Him to - day, hear Him to - day.

Why from the sun - shine of
Bring Him thy bur - den and
Come with thy sins, at His
Those who be - lieve on His

JESUS, LOVER OF MY SOUL

Words by CHARLES WESLEY
Music by SIMEON B. MARSH

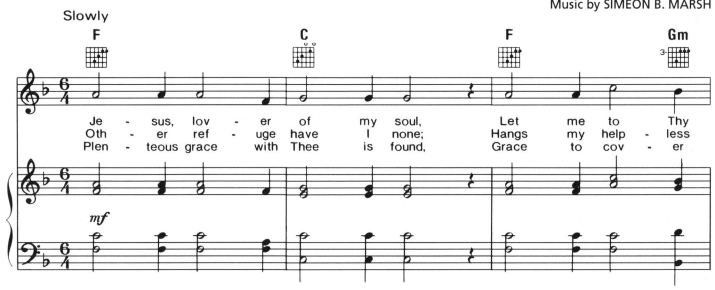

Je - sus, lov - er of my soul, Let me to Thy
Oth - er ref - uge have Thee I none; Hangs my help - less
Plen - teous grace with Thee is found, Grace to cov - er

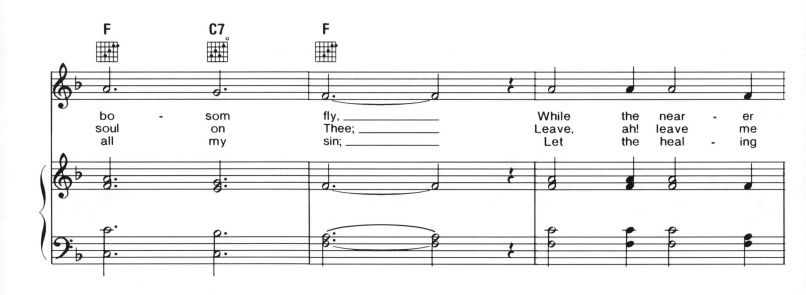

bo - som fly, _____ While the near - er
soul on Thee; _____ Leave, ah! leave me
all my sin; _____ Let the heal - ing

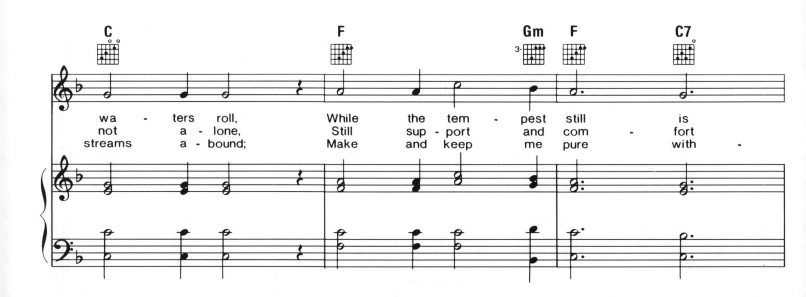

wa - ters roll, While the tem - pest still is
not a - lone, Still sup - port and com - fort
streams a - bound; Make and keep me pure with -

JESUS SAVES!

Words by PRISCILLA J. OWENS
Music by WILLIAM J. KIRKPATRICK

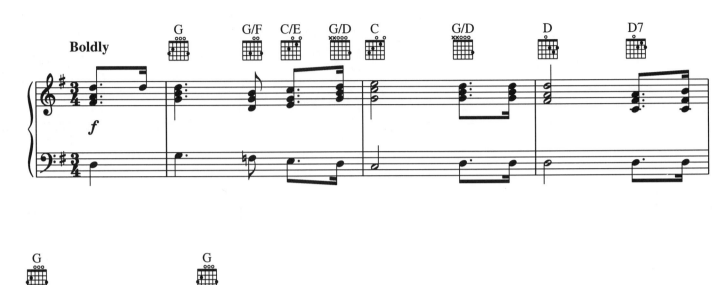

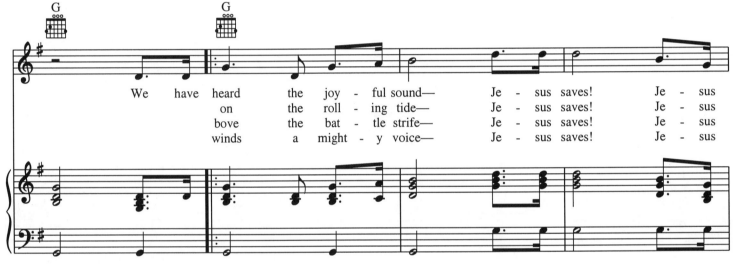

We have heard the joy - ful sound— Je - sus saves! Je - sus
on the roll - ing tide— Je - sus saves! Je - sus
bove the bat - tle strife— Je - sus saves! Je - sus
winds a might - y voice— Je - sus saves! Je - sus

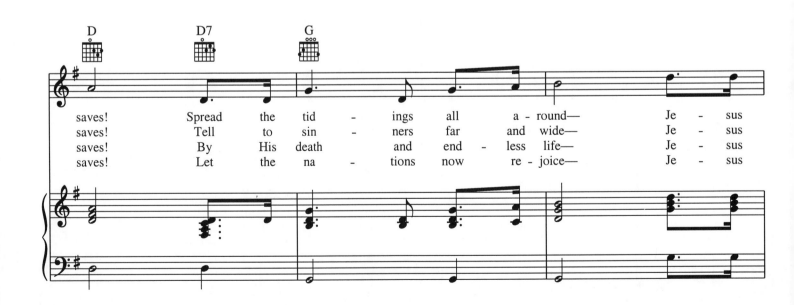

saves! Spread the tid - ings all a - round— Je - sus
saves! Tell to sin - ners far and wide— Je - sus
saves! By His death and end - less life— Je - sus
saves! Let the na - tions now re - joice— Je - sus

saves! Je - sus saves! Bear the news to ev - 'ry land, Climb the
saves! Je - sus saves! Sing, ye is - lands of the sea! Ech - o
saves! Je - sus saves! Sing it soft - ly thru the gloom, When the
saves! Je - sus saves! Shout sal - va - tion full and free, High - est

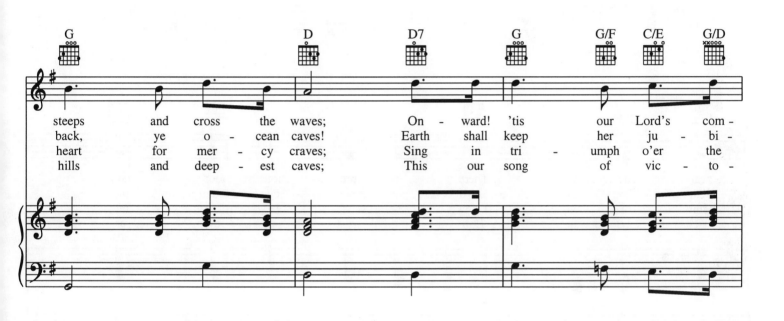

steeps and cross the waves; On - ward! 'tis our Lord's com -
back, ye o - cean caves! Earth shall keep her ju - bi -
heart for mer - cy craves; Sing in tri - umph o'er the
hills and deep - est caves; This our song of vic - to -

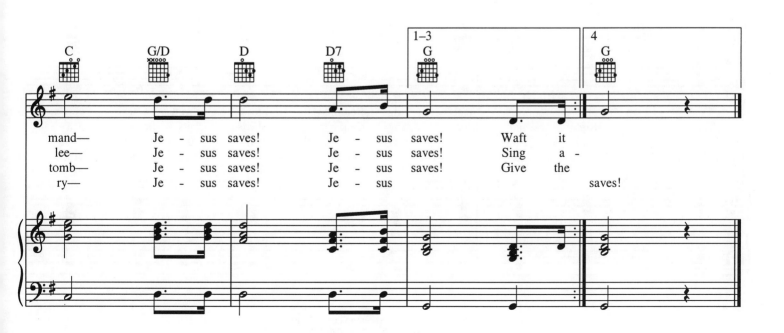

mand— Je - sus saves! Je - sus saves! Waft it
lee— Je - sus saves! Je - sus saves! Sing a -
tomb— Je - sus saves! Je - sus saves! Give the
ry— Je - sus saves! Je - sus saves!

JESUS, KEEP ME NEAR THE CROSS

Words by FANNY J. CROSBY
Music by WILLIAM H. DOANE

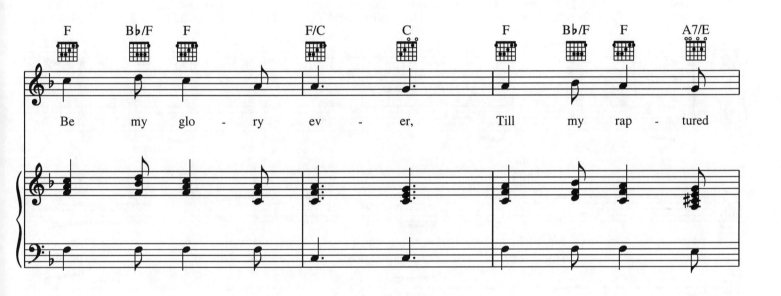

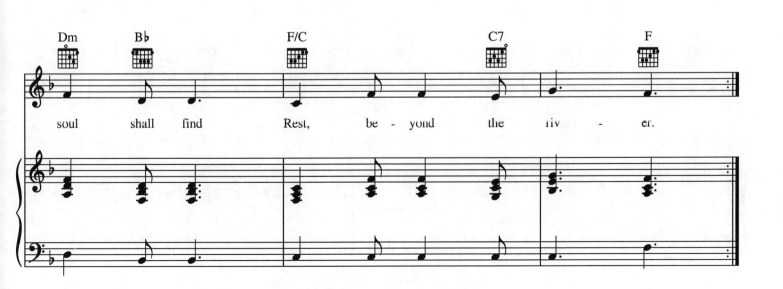

JESUS, SAVIOR, PILOT ME

Words by EDWARD HOPPER
Music by JOHN E. GOULD

JESUS, THOU JOY OF LOVING HEARTS

Words attributed to BERNARD OF CLAIRVAUX
Music by HENRY BAKER

JOYFUL, JOYFUL, WE ADORE THEE

Words by HENRY VAN DYKE
Music by LUDWIG VAN BEETHOVEN,
melody from Ninth Symphony
Adapted by EDWARD HODGES

JUST AS I AM

Words by CHARLOTTE ELLIOTT
Music by WILLIAM BRADBURY

Slowly, with movement

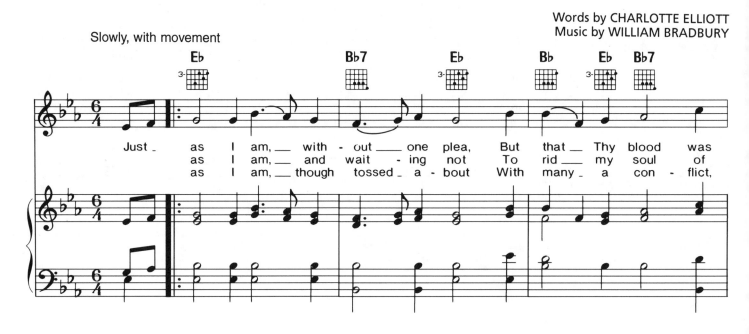

Just _ as I am, __ with - out __ one plea, But that __ Thy blood was
as I am, __ and wait - ing not To rid __ my soul of
as I am, __ though tossed _ a - bout With many _ a con - flict,

shed for me, And _ that Thou bidd'st __ me come to Thee, __ O
one dark blot, To __ Thee whose blood __ can cleanse, each spot, __ O
many a doubt, Fight - ings and fears __ with - in, with - out __ O

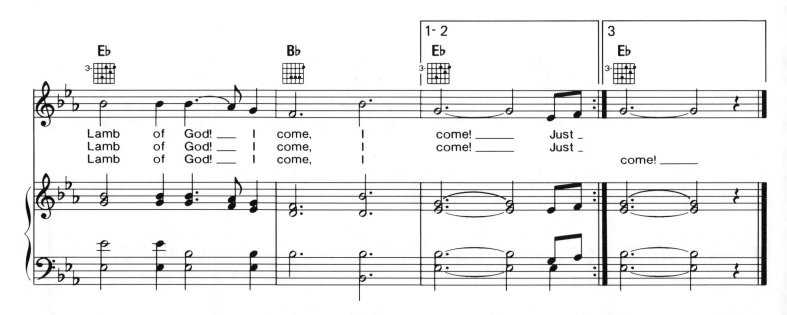

Lamb of God! __ I come, I __ come! ___ Just _
Lamb of God! __ I come, I __ come! ___ Just _
Lamb of God! __ I come, I __ come! ___

LEANING ON THE EVERLASTING ARMS

Words and Music by ELISHA A. HOFFMAN
and A.J. SHOWALTER

Confidently

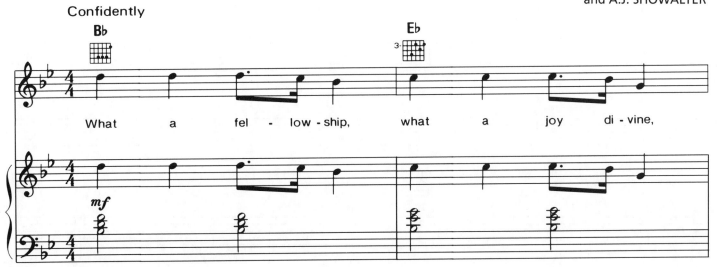

What a fel - low - ship, what a joy di - vine,

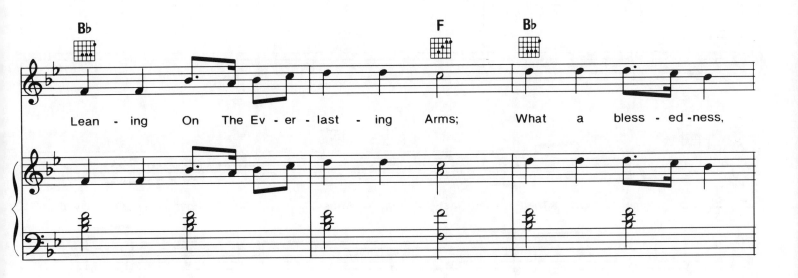

Lean - ing On The Ev - er - last - ing Arms; What a bless - ed - ness,

what a peace is mine, Lean - ing On The Ev - er - last - ing Arms.

LEAD ON, O KING ETERNAL

Words by ERNEST W. SHURTLEFF
Music by HENRY T. SMART

Lead on, O King e - ter - nal, The
on, O King e - ter - nal, Till
on, O King e - ter - nal, We

day of march has come; Hence - forth in fields of
sin's fierce war shall cease, And ho - li - ness shall
fol - low, not with fears; For glad - ness breaks like

LET US BREAK BREAD TOGETHER

African-American Spiritual

LORD, I WANT TO BE A CHRISTIAN

Traditional Negro Spiritual

THE LILY OF THE VALLEY

Words by CHARLES W. FRY
Music by WILLIAM S. HAYS

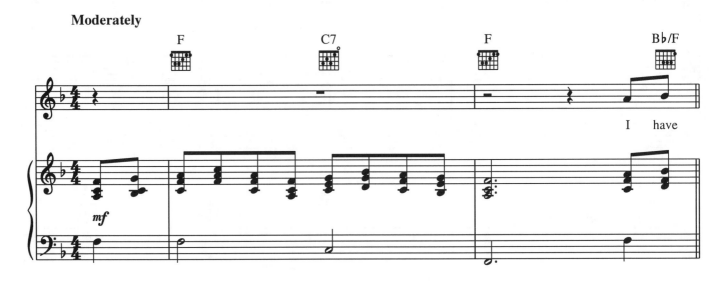

I have

found a friend in Je - sus, He's ev - 'ry - thing to me, He's the
all my grief has tak - en, and all my sor - rows borne; In temp -
nev - er, nev - er leave me, nor yet for - sake me here, While I

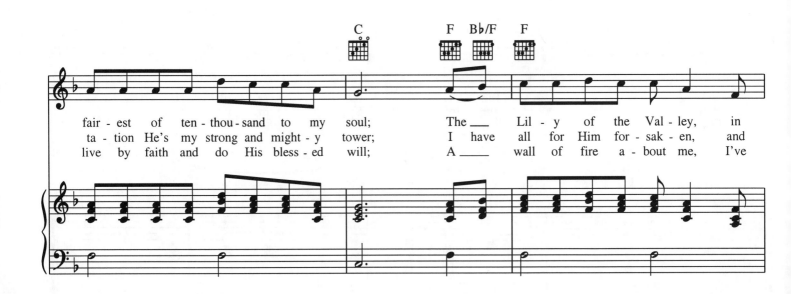

fair - est of ten - thou - sand to my soul; The ___ Lil - y of the Val - ley, in
ta - tion He's my strong and might - y tower; I have all for Him for - sak - en, and
live by faith and do His bless - ed will; A ___ wall of fire a - bout me, I've

THE LORD'S MY SHEPHERD, I'LL NOT WANT

Text based on *Scottish Psalter*, 1650
Music by JESSIE S. IRVINE

LOVE DIVINE, ALL LOVES EXCELLING

Words by CHARLES WESLEY
Music by JOHN ZUNDEL

LOVE LIFTED ME

Words and Music by JAMES ROWE
and HOWARD E. SMITH

A MIGHTY FORTRESS IS OUR GOD

Words and Music by
MARTIN LUTHER

3. And tho this world, with devils filled,
   Should threaten to undo us;
   We will not fear, for God hath willed
   His truth to triumph through us;
   The Prince of darkness grim,
   We tremble not for him;
   His rage we can endure,
   For lo! His doom is sure,
   One little word shall fell him.

4. That word above all earthly powers,
   No thanks to them abideth,
   The spirit and the gifts are ours
   Through Him who with us sideth;
   Let goods and kindred go,
   This mortal life also;
   The body they may kill;
   God's truth abideth still,
   His kingdom is forever.

MY FAITH HAS FOUND A RESTING PLACE

Words by LIDIE H. EDMUNDS
Music by ANDRÉ GRÉTRY

Moderately slow

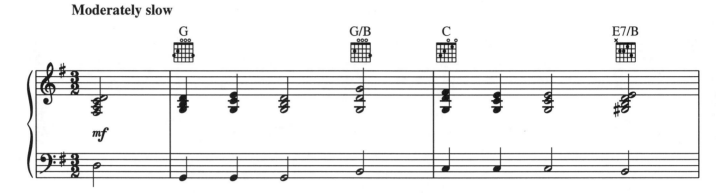

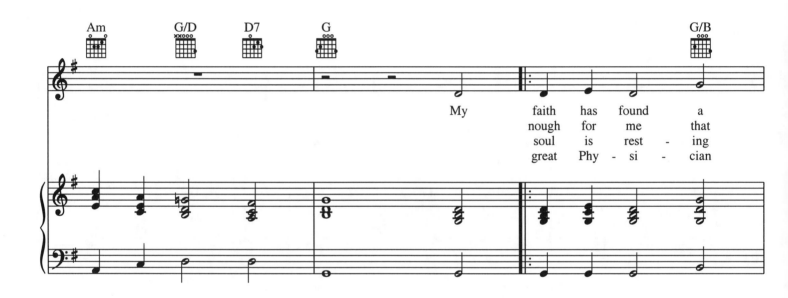

My faith has found a
nough for me that
soul is rest - ing
great Phy - si - cian

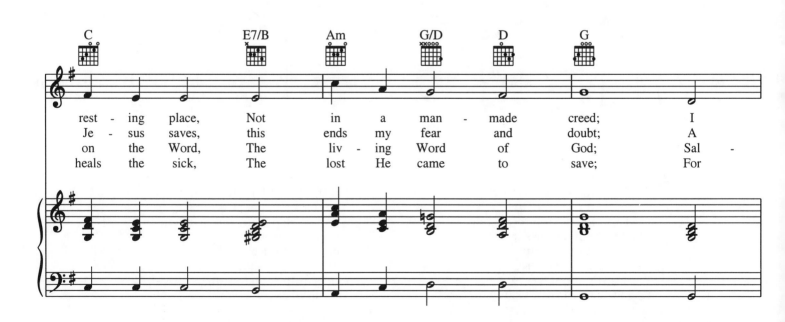

rest - ing place, Not in a man - made creed; I
Je - sus saves, This ends my fear and doubt; A
on the Word, The liv - ing Word of God; Sal -
heals the sick, The lost He came to save; For

MY FAITH LOOKS UP TO THEE

Words by RAY PALMER
Music by LOWELL MASON

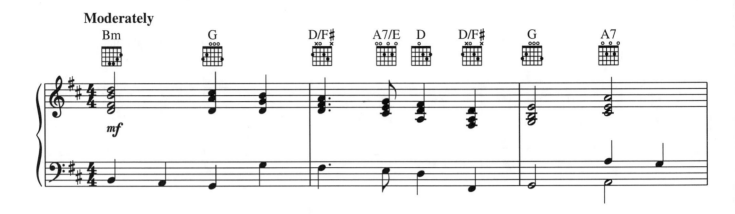

My faith looks up to Thee,
May Thy rich grace im - part
While life's dark maze I tread
When ends life's pass - ing dream,

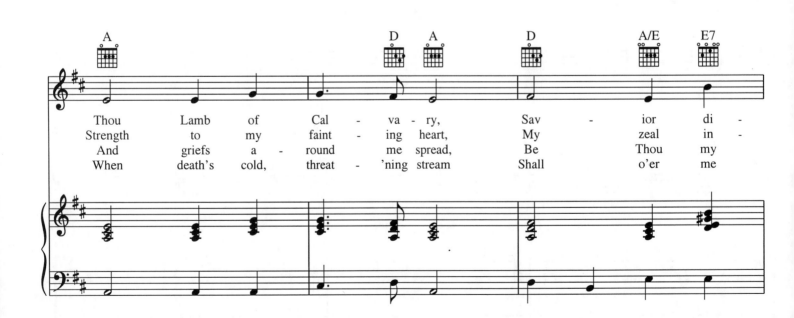

Thou Lamb of Cal - va - ry,   Sav - ior di -
Strength to my faint - ing heart,   My zeal in -
And griefs a - round me spread,   Be Thou my
When death's cold, threat - 'ning stream Shall o'er me

MY HOPE IS BUILT
ON NOTHING LESS

Words by EDWARD MOTE
Music by WILLIAM B. BRADBURY

NEARER, MY GOD, TO THEE

Text by SARAH F. ADAMS
Music by LOWELL MASON

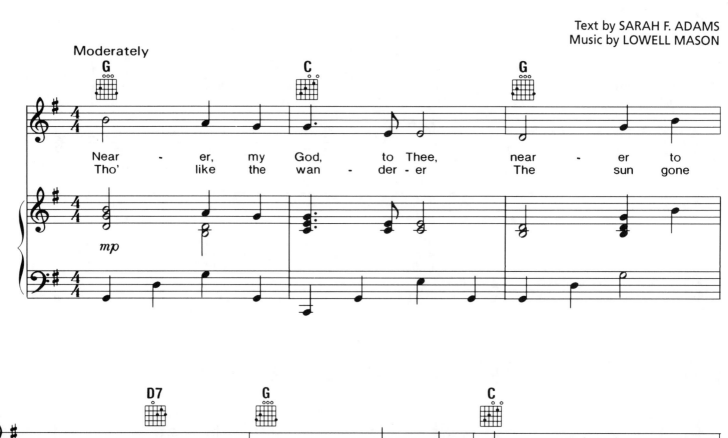

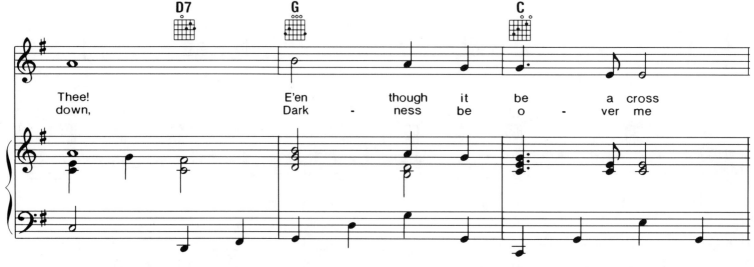

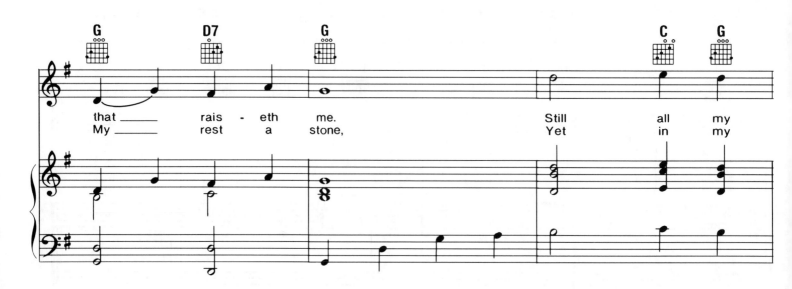

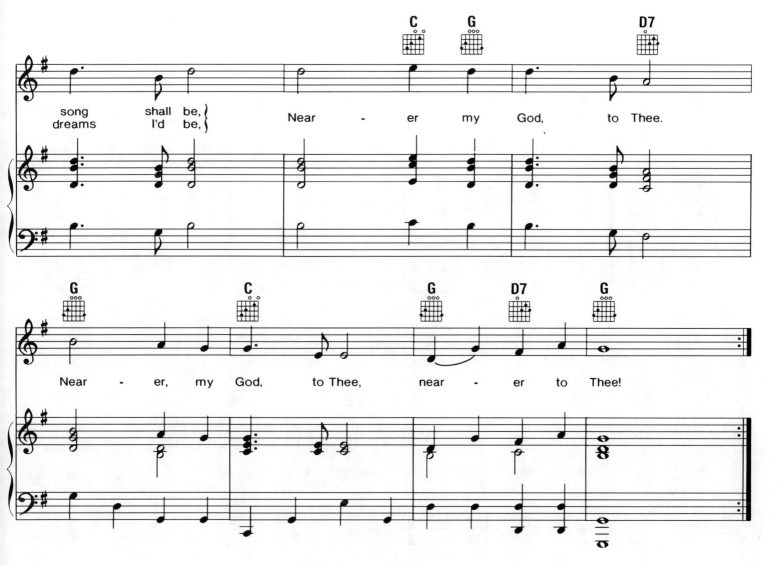

3. Then with my waking tho'ts
   Bright with Thy praise,
   Out of my stony griefs
   Bethel I'll raise
   So by my woes to be,
   Nearer, my God, to Thee,
   Nearer, my God, to Thee,
   Nearer to Thee!

4. Or if on joyful wing,
   Cleaving the sky,
   Sun, moon, and stars forgot,
   Upwards I'll fly,
   Still all my song shall be,
   Nearer, my God, to Thee,
   Nearer, my God, to Thee,
   Nearer to Thee!

NOW THANK WE ALL OUR GOD

German Words by MARTIN RINKART
English Translation by CATHERINE WINKWORTH
Music by JOHANN CRÜGER

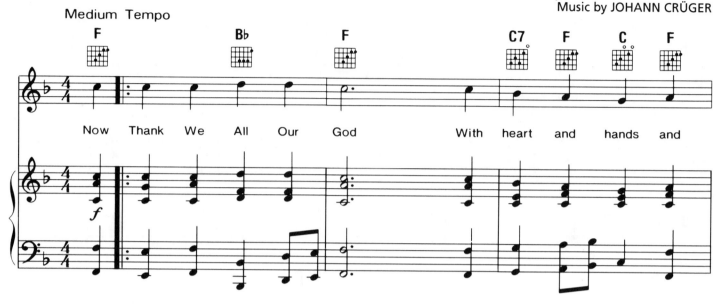

Now Thank We All Our God With heart and hands and

voic - es, Who won - drous things hath done, In

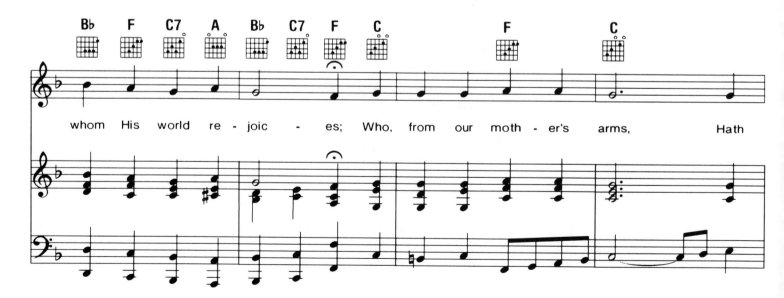

whom His world re - joic - es; Who, from our moth - er's arms, Hath

blessed us on our way   With count - less gifts of

love,   And still is ours to - day.   O more.

2. (O) may this bounteous God
   Through all our life be near us,
   With ever joyful hearts
   And blessed peace to cheer us;
   And keep us in His grace,
   And guide us when perplexed,
   And free us from all ills,
   In this world and the next.

3. (All) praise and thanks to God
   The Father now be given,
   The Son and Him who reigns
   With them in highest heaven;
   The one eternal God,
   Whom earth and heav'n adore;
   For thus it was, is now,
   And shall be evermore.

NOW THE DAY IS OVER

Words by SABINE BARING-GOULD
Music by JOSEPH BARNBY

O FOR A THOUSAND TONGUES TO SING

Text by CHARLES WESLEY
Music by CARL G. GLÄSER

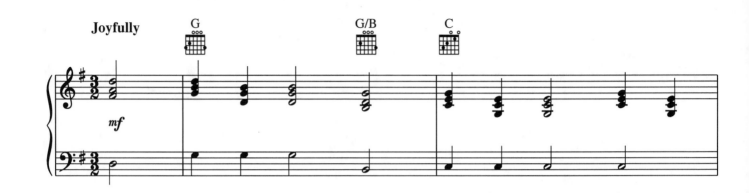

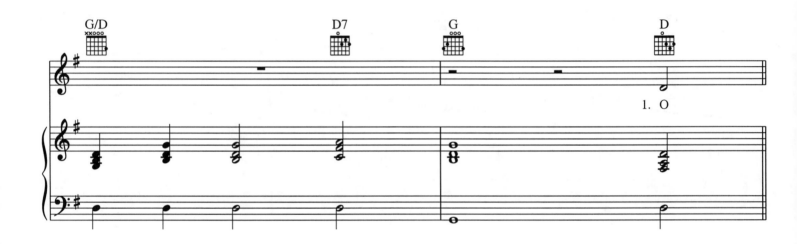

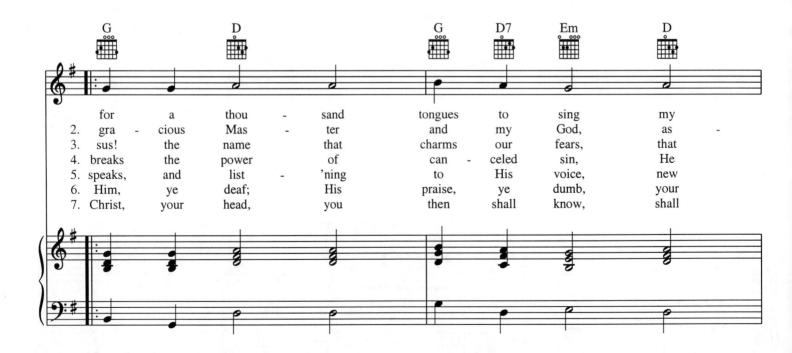

for	a	thou -	sand	tongues	to	sing	my
2. gra -	cious	Mas -	ter	and	my	God,	as -
3. sus!	the	name	that	charms	our	fears,	that
4. breaks	the	power	of	can - celed	sin,		He
5. speaks,	and	list -	'ning	to	His	voice,	new
6. Him,	ye	deaf;	His	praise,	ye	dumb,	your
7. Christ,	your	head,	you	then	shall	know,	shall

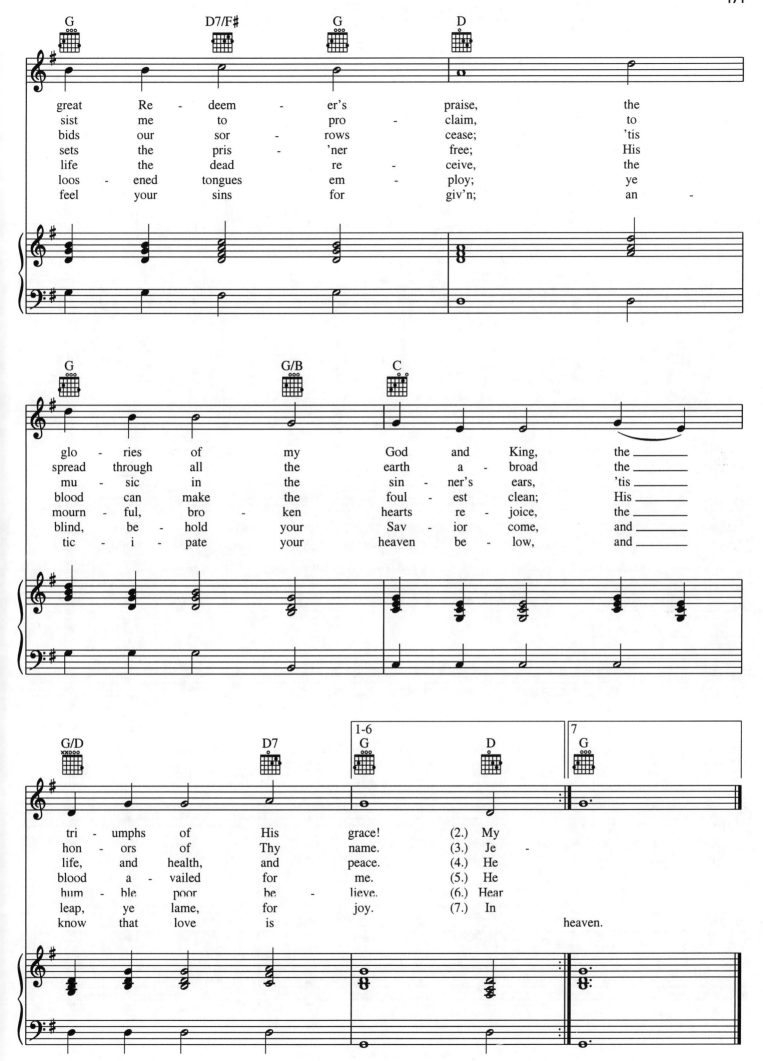

O GOD, OUR HELP IN AGES PAST

Words by ISAAC WATTS
Melody attributed to WILLIAM CROFT

O JESUS, I HAVE PROMISED

Words by JOHN E. BODE
Music by ARTHUR H. MANN

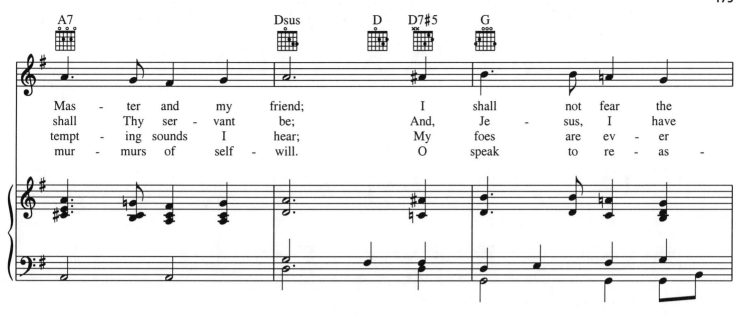

Master and my friend; I shall not fear the
shall Thy ser - vant be; And, Je - sus, I have
tempt - ing sounds I hear; My foes are ev - er
mur - murs of self - will. O speak to re - as -

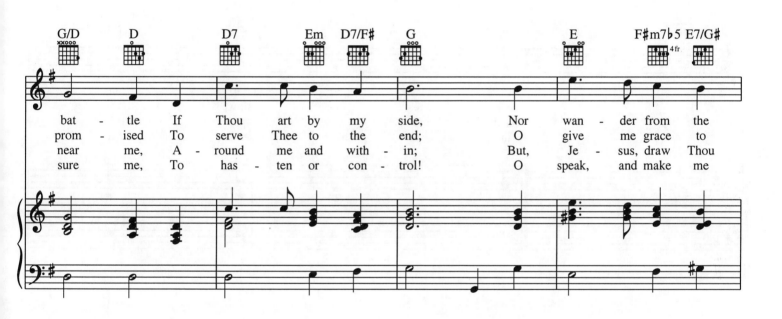

bat - tle If Thou art by my side, Nor wan - der from the
prom - ised To serve Thee to the end; O give me grace to
near me, A - round me and with - in; But, Je - sus, draw Thou
sure me, To has - ten or con - trol! O speak, and make me

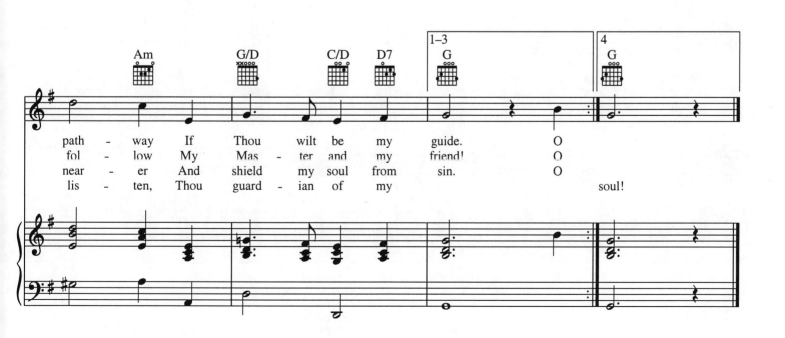

path - way If Thou wilt be my guide. O
fol - low My Mas - ter and my friend! O
near - er And shield my soul from sin. O
lis - ten, Thou guard - ian of my soul!

O MASTER, LET ME WALK WITH THEE

Words by WASHINGTON GLADDEN
Music by H. PERCY SMITH

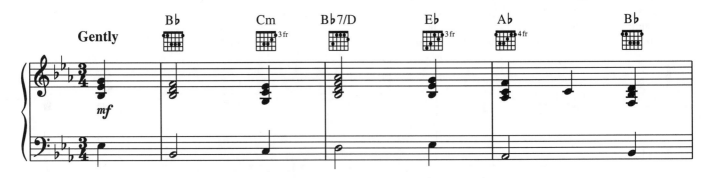

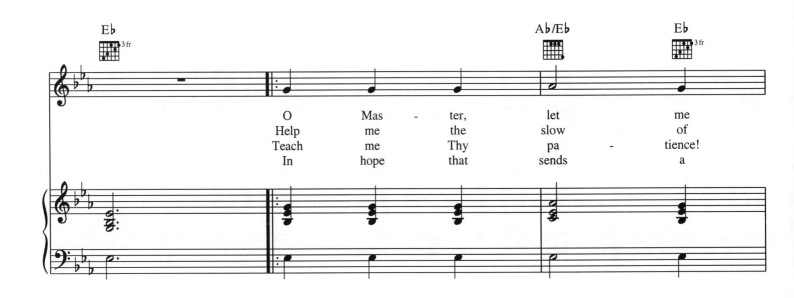

O Mas - ter, let me
Help me the slow of
Teach me Thy pa - tience!
In hope that sends a

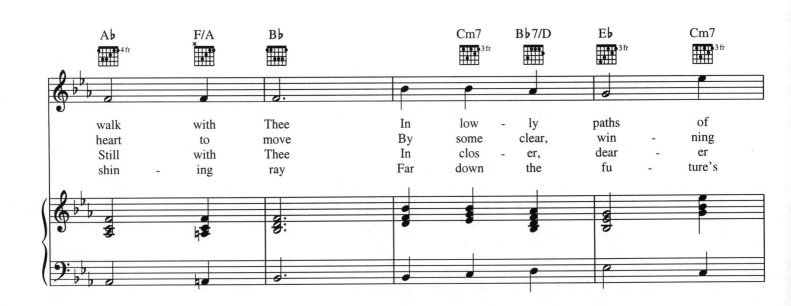

walk with Thee In low - ly paths of
heart to move By some clear, win - ning
Still with Thee In clos - er, dear - er
shin - ing ray Far down the fu - ture's

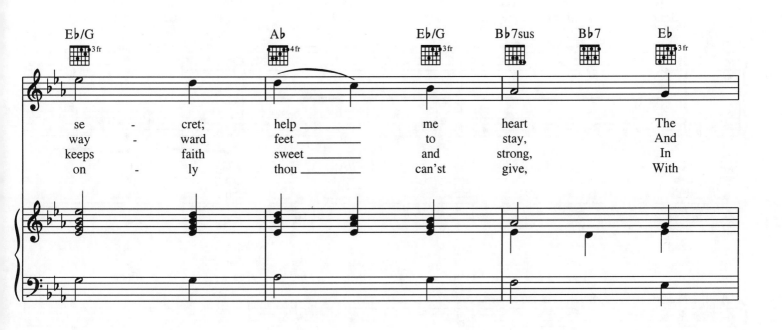

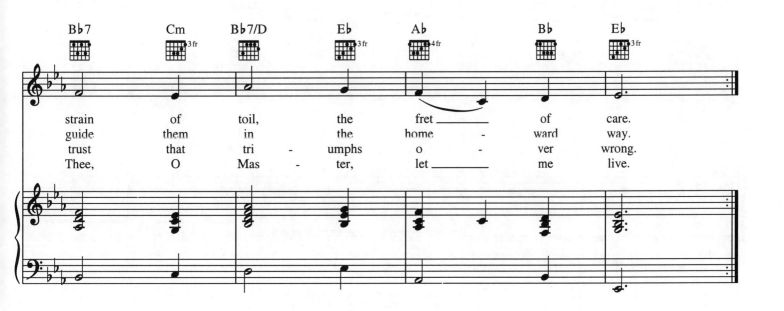

O PERFECT LOVE

Words by DOROTHY FRANCES GURNEY
Music by JOSEPH BARNBY

O SACRED HEAD, NOW WOUNDED

Words by BERNARD OF CLAIRVAUX
Music by HANS HASSLER

O WORSHIP THE KING

Words by ROBERT GRANT
Based on "Lyons,"
Attributed to JOHANN MICHAEL HAYDN

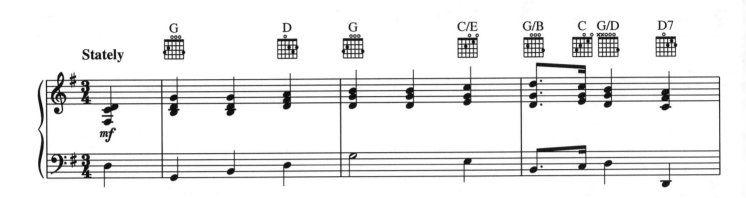

O
wor - ship the King, all glo - rious a -
tell of His might, and sing of His
boun - ti - ful care, what tongue can re -
chil - dren of dust, and fee - ble as

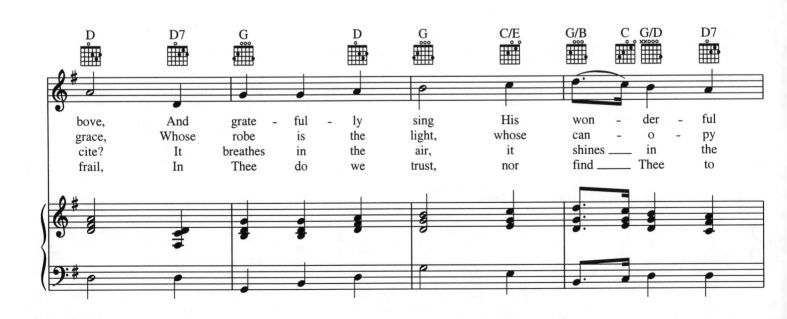

bove, And grate - ful - ly sing His won - der - ful
grace, Whose robe is the light, whose can - o - py
cite? It breathes in the air, it shines in the
frail, In Thee do we trust, nor find Thee to

OH, HOW I LOVE JESUS

Words by FREDERICK WHITFIELD
Traditional American Melody

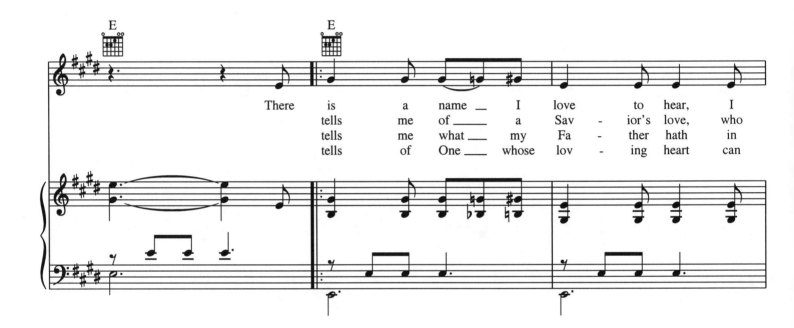

There is a name __ I love to hear, I
tells me of ___ a Sav - ior's love, who
tells me what ___ my Fa - ther hath in
tells of One ___ whose lov - ing heart can

love to sing __ its worth; _____ It sounds like mu - sic
died to set ___ me free; _____ It tells me of ___ His
store for ev - 'ry day; _____ And though I tread ___ a
feel my deep - est woe, _____ Who in each sor - row

THE OLD RUGGED CROSS

By REV. GEORGE BENNARD

ON JORDAN'S STORMY BANKS

Words by SAMUEL STENNETT
American Folk Hymn
Arranged by RIGDON M. McINTOSH

ONCE TO EVERY MAN AND NATION

Words by JAMES RUSSELL LOWELL
Music by THOMAS J. WILLIAMS

ONLY TRUST HIM

Words and Music by
JOHN H. STOCKTON

Come, ev - 'ry soul by sin op -pressed, There's mer - cy with the
Je - sus shed His pre - cious blood, Rich bless - ings to be

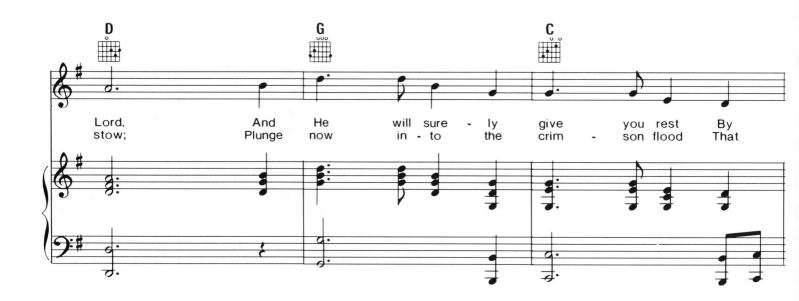

Lord, And He will sure - ly give you rest By
stow; Plunge now in - to the crim - son flood That

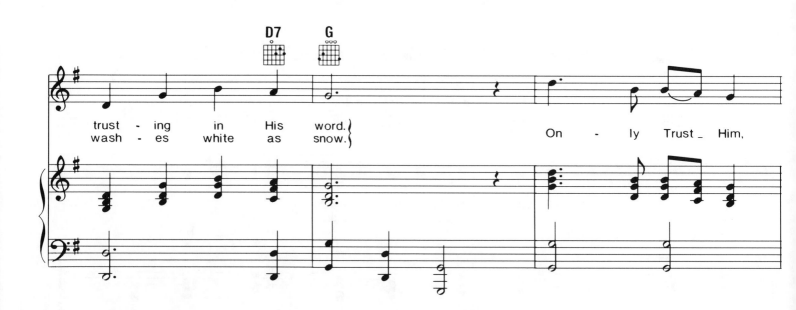

trust - ing in His word.
wash - es white as snow.

On - ly Trust Him,

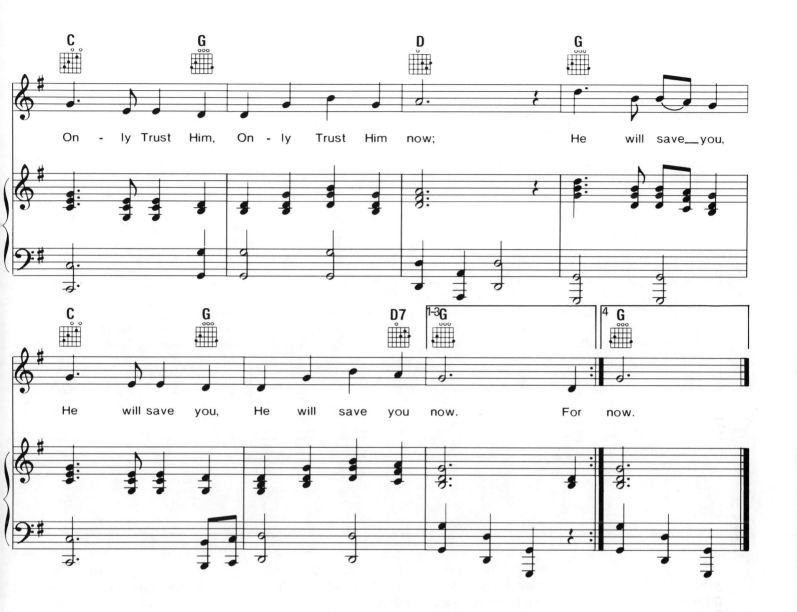

On - ly Trust Him, On - ly Trust Him now; He will save__you,

He will save you, He will save you now. For now.

3. Yes, Jesus is the truth, the way,
That leads you into rest;
Believe in Him without delay,
And you are fully blest.

4. Come, then, and join this holy band,
And on to glory go,
To dwell in that celestial land,
Where joys immortal flow.

ONWARD, CHRISTIAN SOLDIERS

Words by SABINE BARING-GOULD
Music by ARTHUR S. SULLIVAN

OPEN MY EYES, THAT I MAY SEE

Words and Music by CLARA H. SCOTT

PASS ME NOT, O GENTLE SAVIOR

Words by FANNY J. CROSBY
Music by WILLIAM H. DOANE

1. Pass me not, O gen - tle
2.-4. *(See additional verses)*

Sav - ior, hear my hum - ble cry;

While on oth - ers Thou art call - ing, do not pass me

Refrain

by. Sav - ior, Sav - ior, hear my hum - ble cry; While on oth - ers Thou art call - ing, do not pass me by. by.

Additional Verses

2. Let me at the throne of mercy find a sweet relief;
   Kneeling there in deep contrition, help my unbelief.
   REFRAIN

3. Trusting only in Thy merit, would I seek Thy face;
   Heal my wounded, broken spirit, save me by Thy grace.
   REFRAIN

4. Be the Spring of all my comfort, more than life to me;
   Not just here on earth beside me, but eternally.
   REFRAIN

PRAISE GOD, FROM WHOM ALL BLESSINGS FLOW

Words by THOMAS KEN
Music Attributed to LOUIS BOURGEOIS

PRAISE TO THE LORD, THE ALMIGHTY

Words by JOACHIM NEANDER
Music from *Erneuerten Gesangbuch*
Harmony by WILLIAM STERNDALE BENNETT

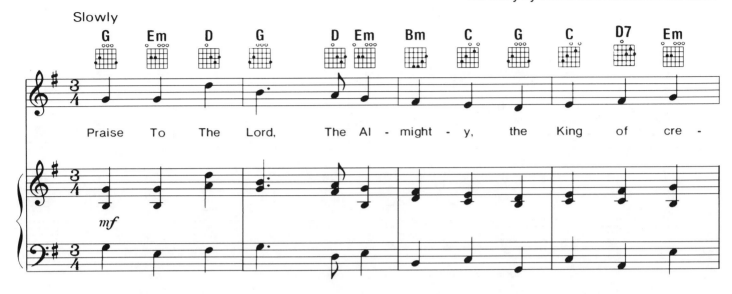

Praise To The Lord, The Al - might - y, the King of cre -

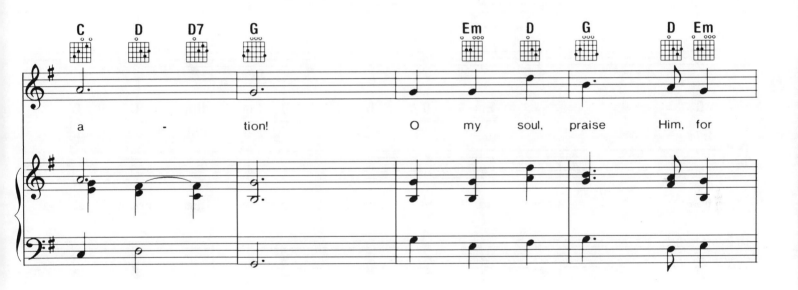

a - tion! O my soul, praise Him, for

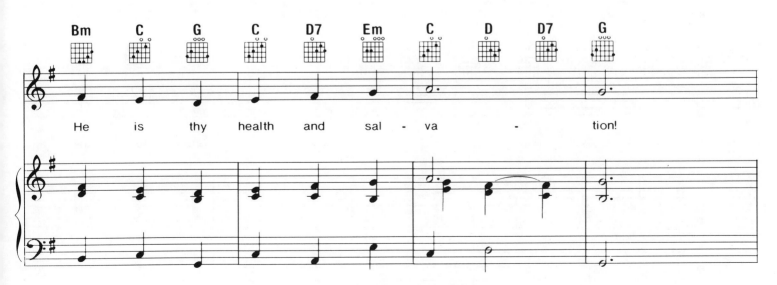

He is thy health and sal - va - tion!

REDEEMED

Words by FANNY J. CROSBY
Music by WILLIAM J. KIRKPATRICK

deemed, how I love to pro - claim it! Re - deemed by the blood of the
deemed and so hap - py in Je - sus, No lan - guage my rap - ture can
think of my bless - ed Re - deem - er, I think of Him all the day
know I shall see in His beau - ty The King in whose law I de -

Lamb; _____ Re - deemed through His in - fi - nite mer - cy, His
tell; _____ I know that the light of His pres - ence With
long; _____ I sing, for I can - not be si - lent; His
light; _____ Who lov - ing - ly guard - eth my foot - steps, And

ROCK OF AGES

Text by AUGUSTUS M. TOPLADY
Music by THOMAS HASTINGS

3. While I draw this fleeting breath,
When my eyes shall close in death,
When I rise to worlds unknown,
And behold Thee on Thy throne,
Rock Of Ages cleft for me,
Let me hide myself in Thee.

SAVIOR, LIKE A SHEPHERD LEAD US

Words attributed to DOROTHY A. THRUPP
Music by WILLIAM B. BRADBURY

Quietly

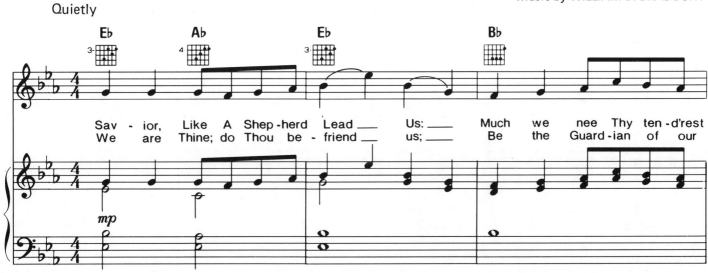

Sav - ior, Like A Shep -herd Lead ___ Us: ___ Much we nee Thy ten -d'rest
We are Thine; do Thou be - friend ___ us; ___ Be the Guard -ian of our

care; In Thy pleas -ant pas -tures feed ____ us, ____
way; Keep Thy flock, from sin de - fend ____ us, ____

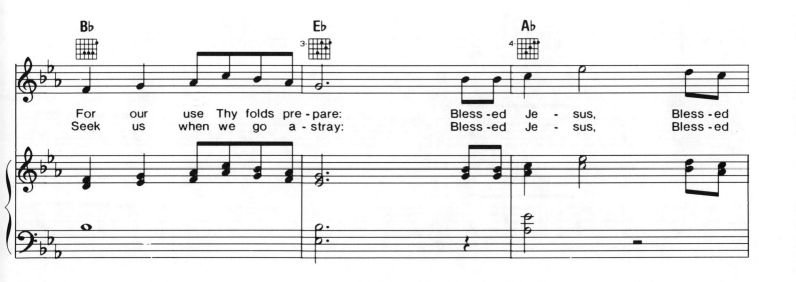

For our use Thy folds pre - pare: Bless -ed Je - sus, Bless -ed
Seek us when we go a -stray: Bless -ed Je - sus, Bless -ed

SHALL WE GATHER AT THE RIVER?

Words and Music by
ROBERT LOWRY

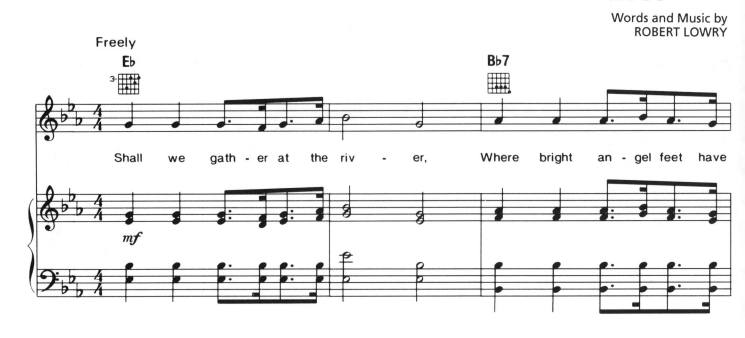

Shall we gath-er at the riv-er, Where bright an-gel feet have

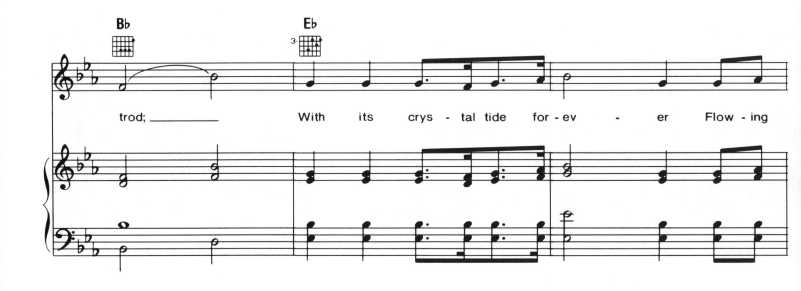

trod; _____ With its crys-tal tide for-ev-er Flow-ing

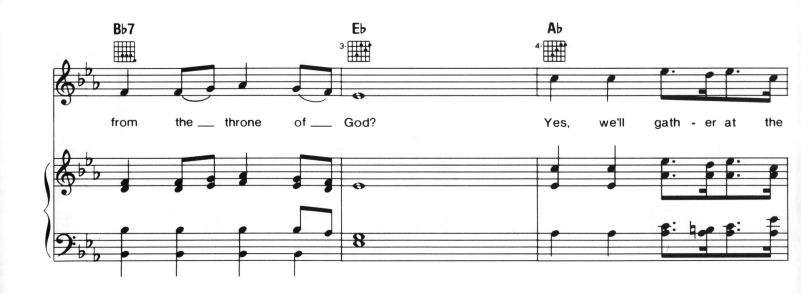

from the __ throne of __ God? Yes, we'll gath-er at the

riv - er, The beau - ti - ful, the beau - ti - ful ___ riv - er,

Gath - er with the saints _ at the riv - er, That flows from the throne of _ God.

2. On the margin of the river,
   Washing up its silver spray,
   We shall walk and worship ever
   All the happy, golden day.

3. On the bosom of the river,
   Where the Saviour King we own,
   We shall meet and sorrow never
   'Neath the glory of the throne.

4. Ere we reach the shining river,
   Lay we ev'ry burden down:
   Grace our spirits will deliver,
   And provide a robe and crown.

5. Soon we'll reach the shining river,
   Soon our pilgrimage will cease;
   Soon our happy hearts will quiver
   With the melody of peace.

SINCE JESUS CAME INTO MY HEART

Words by R.H. McDANIEL
Music by CHARLES H. GABRIEL

Additional Verses

3. There's a light in the valley of death now for me,
Since Jesus came into my heart!
And the gates of the city beyond I can see,
Since Jesus came into my heart!
REFRAIN

4. I shall go there to dwell in that city, I know,
Since Jesus came into my heart!
And I'm happy, so happy, as onward I go,
Since Jesus came into my heart!
REFRAIN

SOFTLY AND TENDERLY

Words and Music by
WILL L. THOMPSON

Moderately Slow

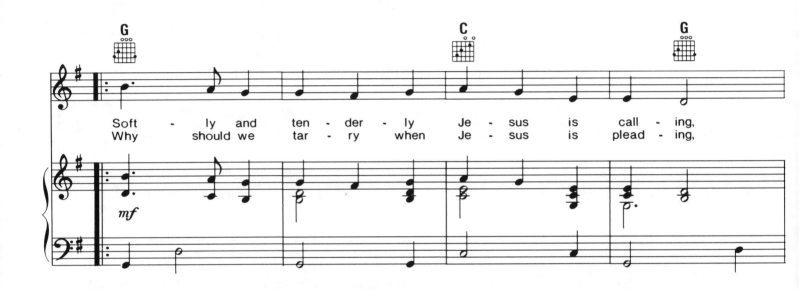

Soft - ly and ten - der - ly Je - sus is call - ing,
Why should we tar - ry when Je - sus is plead - ing,

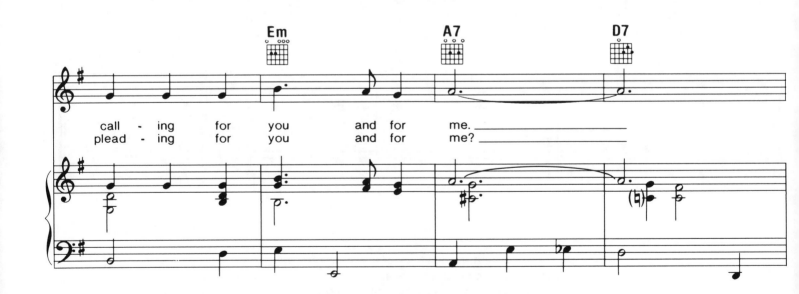

call - ing for you and for me.
plead - ing for you and for me?

SOMEBODY'S KNOCKIN' AT YOUR DOOR

African-American Spiritual

SPIRIT OF GOD, DESCEND UPON MY HEART

Words by GEORGE CROLY
Music by FREDERICK COOK ATKINSON

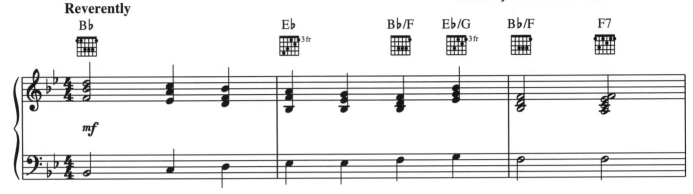

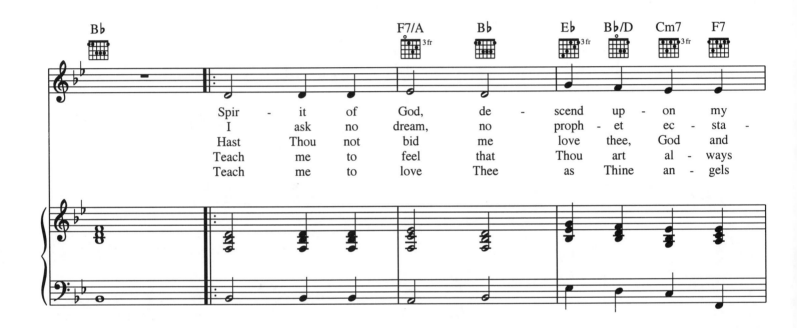

Spir - it of God, de - scend up - on my
I ask no dream, no proph - et ec - sta -
Hast Thou not bid me love thee, God and
Teach me to love Thee as Thine an - gels

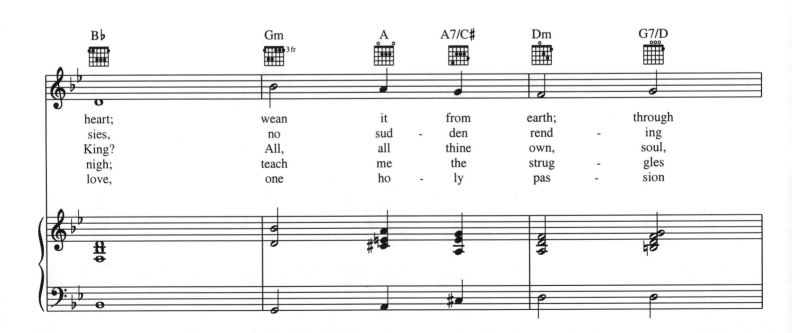

heart; wean it from earth; through
sies, no sud - den rend - ing
King? All, all thine own, soul,
nigh; teach me the strug - gles
love, one ho - ly pas - sion

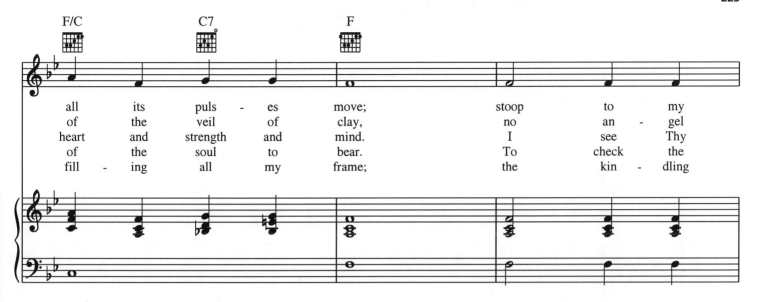

all   its   puls - es   move;   stoop   to   my
of   the   veil   of   clay,   no   an - gel
heart   and   strength and mind.   I   see   Thy
of   the   soul   to   bear.   To   check the
fill - ing   all   my   frame;   the   kin - dling

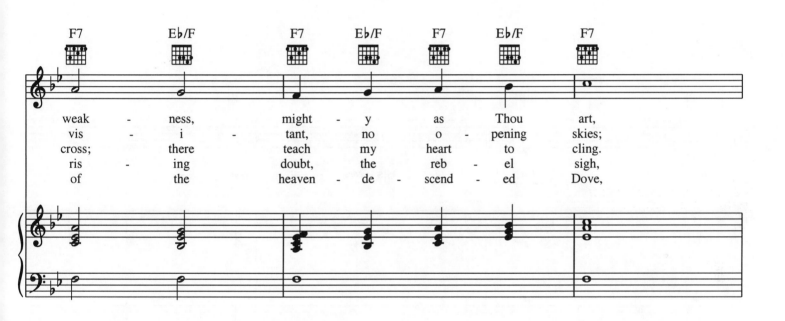

weak - ness,   might - y   as   Thou   art,
vis - i - tant,   no   o - pening skies;
cross;   there   teach my   heart   to   cling.
ris - ing   doubt, the   reb - el   sigh,
of   the   heaven - de - scend - ed   Dove,

and   make   me   love Thee   as   I   ought   to   love.
but   take   the   dim - ness   of   my   soul   a - way.
O   let   me   seek Thee, and O   let   me   find!
teach   me   the   pa - tience of   un - an - swered   prayer.
my   heart an   al - tar,   and Thy love   the   flame.

STAND UP, STAND UP FOR JESUS

Words by GEORGE DUFFIELD, JR.
Music by GEORGE J. WEBB

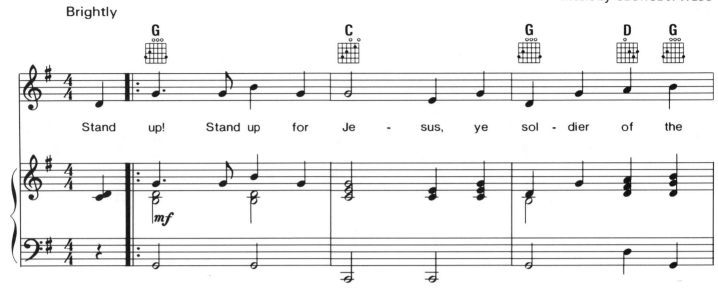

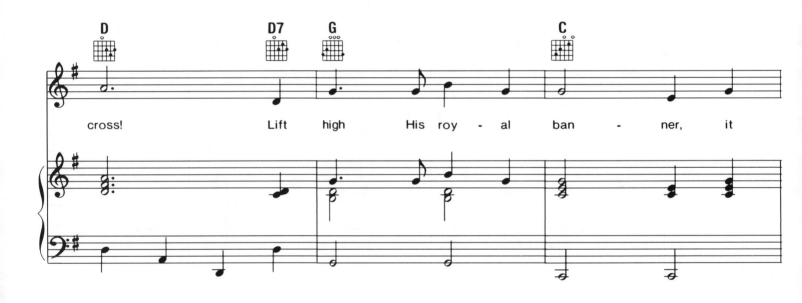

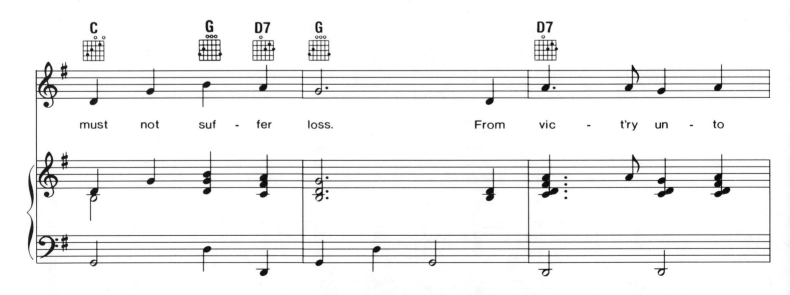

2. Stand up, stand up for Jesus,
   The strife will not be long;
   This day the noise of battle,
   The next, the victor's song;
   To him the overcometh,
   A crown of life shall be;
   He with the King of glory
   Shall reign eternally.

STANDING ON THE PROMISES

Words and Music by
R. KELSO CARTER

Moderately

1. Stand-ing on the prom-is-es of
2.-4. (See additional verses)

Christ my King, Thru e-ter-nal a-ges let His prais-es ring;

Glo-ry in the high-est, I will shout and sing, Stand-ing on the prom-is-es of

Additional Verses

2. Standing on the promises that cannot fail,
When the howling storms of doubt and fear assail,
By the living word of God I shall prevail,
Standing on the promises of God.
REFRAIN

3. Standing on the promises of Christ the Lord,
Bound to Him eternally by love's strong cord,
Overcoming daily with the Spirit's sword,
Standing on the promises of God.
REFRAIN

4. Standing on the promises I cannot fall,
Listening ev'ry moment to the Spirit's call,
Resting in my Savior as my all in all,
Standing on the promises of God.
REFRAIN

SWEET BY AND BY

Words by SANFORD FILLMORE BENNETT
Music by JOSEPH P. WEBSTER

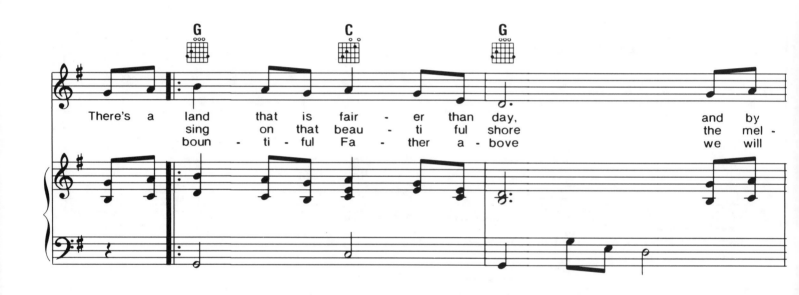

There's a land that is fair - er than day, and by
sing on that beau - ti - ful shore the mel -
boun - ti - ful Fa - ther a - bove we will

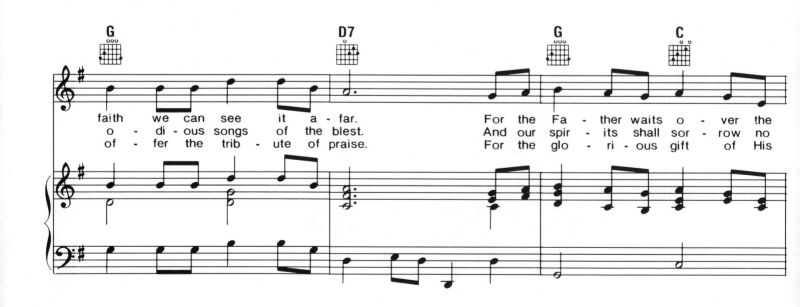

faith we can see it a - far. For the Fa - ther waits o - ver the
o - di - ous songs of the blest. And our spir - its shall sor - row no
of - fer the trib - ute of praise. For the glo - ri - ous gift of His

SWEET HOUR OF PRAYER

Words by WILLIAM W. WALFORD
Music by WILLIAM B. BRADBURY

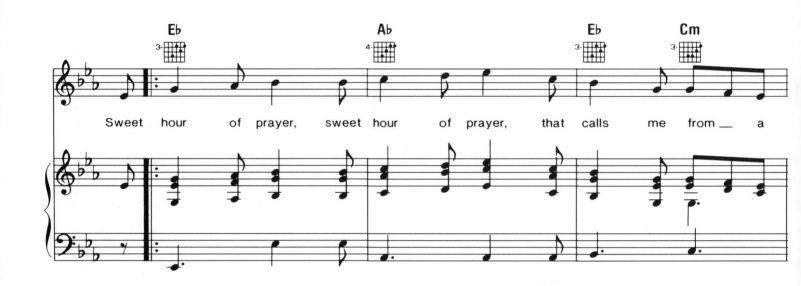

Sweet hour of prayer, sweet hour of prayer, that calls me from __ a

world of care And bids me at my Fa - ther's throne: Make all my wants and

2. (Sweet) hour of prayer,
   Sweet hour of prayer,
   thy wings shall my petition bear
   To Him whose truth and faithfulness
   engage the waiting soul to bless.
   And since He bids me seek His face,
   believe His word, and trust His grace,
   I'll cast on Him my ev-'ry care
   and wait for thee, sweet hour of prayer.

3. (Sweet) hour of prayer,
   sweet hour of prayer,
   may I thy consolation share
   Till from Mount Pisgah's lofty height
   I view my home and take my flight.
   This robe of flesh I'll drop and rise
   to seize the everlasting prize
   And shout while passing through the air
   farewell, farewel', sweet hour of prayer.

TAKE MY LIFE AND LET IT BE CONSECRATED

Words by FRANCES R. HAVERGAL
Music by LOUIS J.F. HÉROLD
Arranged by GEORGE KINGSLEY

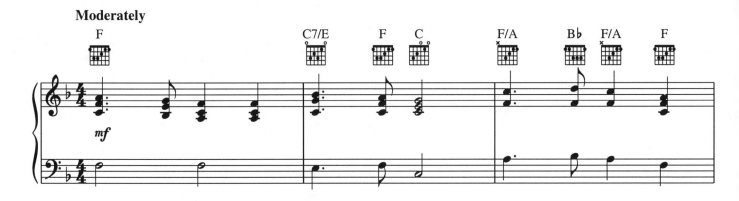

Take my life, and let it be
Take my voice, and let me sing
Take my will and make it Thine;

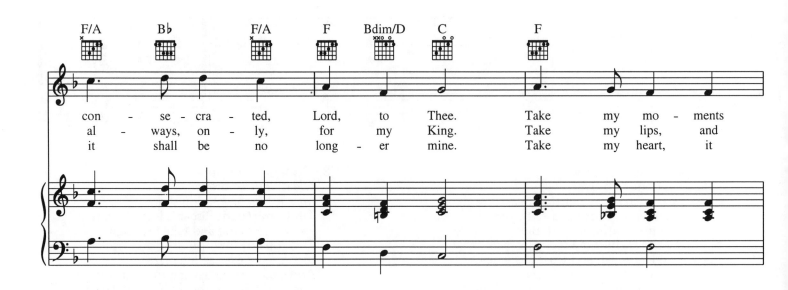

con - se - cra - ted, Lord, to Thee. Take my mo - ments
al - ways, on - ly, for my King. Take my lips, and
it shall be no long - er mine. Take my heart, it

TAKE THE NAME OF JESUS WITH YOU

Words by LYDIA BAXTER
Music by WILLIAM H. DOANE

Take the name of Je - sus with you,
Take the name of Je - sus ev - er
O the pre - cious name of Je - sus!
At the name of Je - sus bow - ing,

Child of sor - row and of woe.
As a shield from ev - 'ry snare.
How it thrills our souls with joy
Fall - ing pros - trate at His feet,

It will joy and com - fort
If temp - ta - tions round you
When His lov - ing arms re -
King of kings in heav'n we'll

TAKE TIME TO BE HOLY

Words by WILLIAM D. LONGSTAFF
Music by GEORGE C. STEBBINS

Take time to be ho - ly, speak oft with thy
Take time to be ho - ly; the world rush - es
Take time to be ho - ly, let Him be thy
Take time to be ho - ly, be calm in thy

Lord,_____ A - bide in Him al - ways
on._____ Spend much time in se - cret
guide,_____ And run not be - fore Him,
soul,_____ Each thought and each mo - tive

THERE IS A BALM IN GILEAD

African-American Spiritual

THERE IS A FOUNTAIN

Words by WILLIAM COWPER
Traditional American Melody
Arranged by LOWELL MASON

Additional Verses

2. The dying thief rejoiced to see
   That fountain in his day;
   And there may I, though vile as he,
   Wash all my sins away:...

3. Dear dying Lamb, Thy precious blood
   Shall never lose its power,
   Till all the ransomed Church of God
   Be saved, to sin no more:...

4. E'er since by faith, I saw the stream
   Thy flowing wounds supply,
   Redeeming love has been my theme,
   And shall be till I die:...

5. Then in a nobler, sweeter song,
   I'll sing Thy power to save,
   When this poor lisping, stamm'ring tongue
   Lies silent in the grave:... Amen.

THERE IS POWER IN THE BLOOD

Words and Music by
LEWIS E. JONES

THIS IS MY FATHER'S WORLD

Words by MALTBIE BABCOCK
Music by FRANKLIN L. SHEPPARD

WERE YOU THERE?

African-American Spiritual
Harmony by CHARLES WINFRED DOUGLAS

Moderately

Were you there when they cru-ci-fied my Lord? (Were you there?) Were you
there when they nailed Him to the tree? (To the tree?) Were you
there when they pierced Him in the side? (In the side?) Were you

there when they cru-ci-fied my Lord? _____ Oh, _____
there when they nailed Him to the tree? _____ Oh, _____
there when they pierced Him in the side? _____ Oh, _____

'TIS SO SWEET TO TRUST IN JESUS

Words by LOUISA M.R. STEAD
Music by WILLIAM J. KIRKPATRICK

saith   the   Lord."
cleans - ing   flood!
joy   and   peace.
to   the   end.

Je - sus,   Je - sus,   how   I   trust   Him!

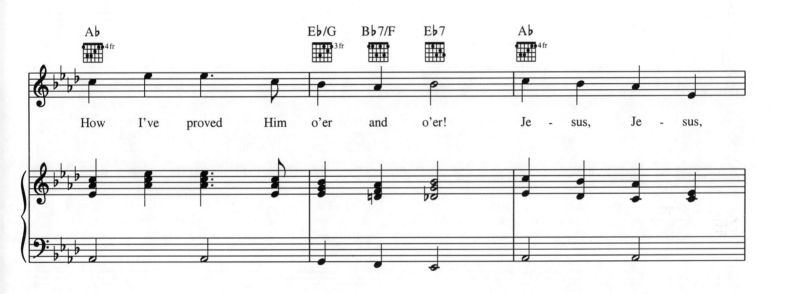

How   I've   proved   Him   o'er   and   o'er!   Je - sus,   Je - sus,

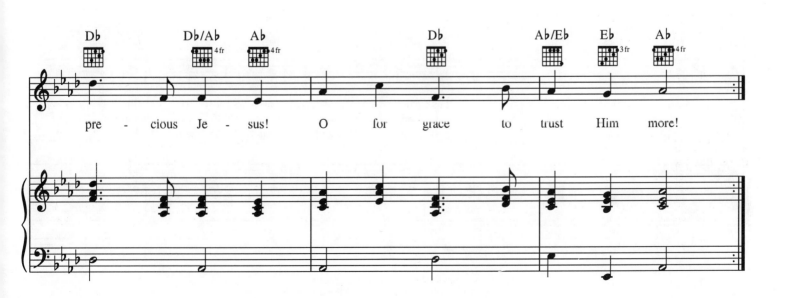

pre - cious Je - sus!   O   for   grace   to   trust   Him   more!

TO GOD BE THE GLORY

Words by FANNY J. CROSBY
Music by WILLIAM H. DOANE

TRUST AND OBEY

Words by JOHN H. SAMMIS
Music by DANIEL B. TOWNER

WE GATHER TOGETHER

Netherlands Folk Hymn

WE'RE MARCHING TO ZION

Words by ISAAC WATTS
Music by ROBERT LOWRY

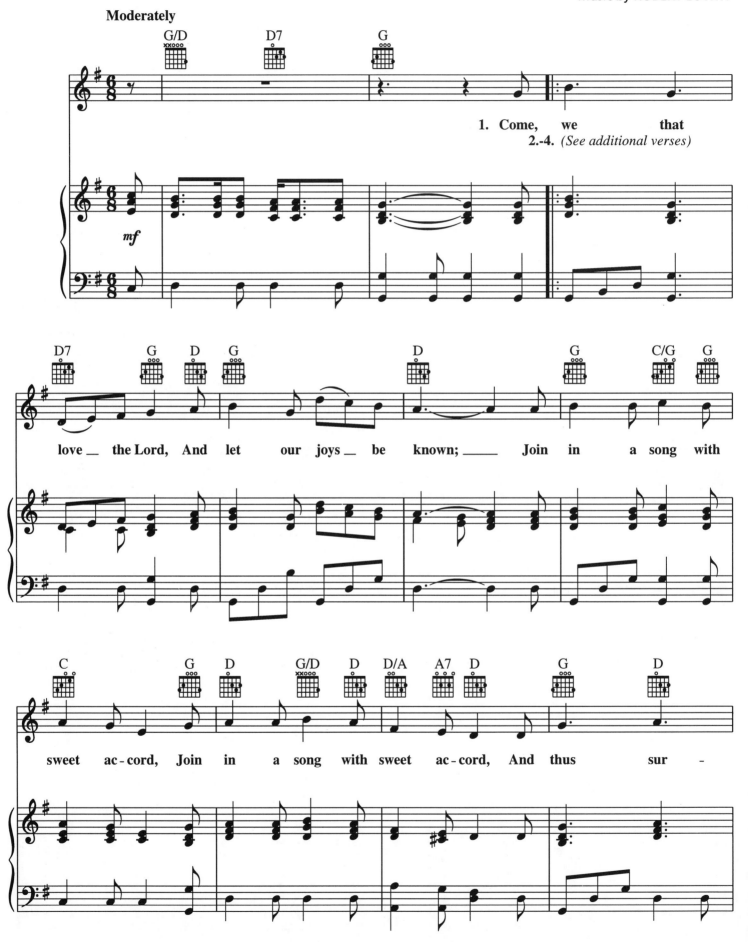

Additional Verses

2. Let those refuse to sing
   Who never knew our God;
   But children of the heav'nly King,
   But children of the heav'nly King,
   May speak their joys abroad,
   May speak their joys abroad.
   REFRAIN

3. The hill of Zion yields
   A thousand sacred sweets,
   Before we reach the heav'nly fields,
   Before we reach the heav'nly fields,
   Or walk the golden streets,
   Or walk the golden streets.
   REFRAIN

4. Then let our songs abound,
   And ev'ry tear be dry;
   We're marching thru Immanuel's ground,
   We're marching thru Immanuel's ground,
   To fairer worlds on high,
   To fairer worlds on high.
   REFRAIN

WHAT A FRIEND WE HAVE IN JESUS

Words by JOSEPH SCRIVEN
Music by CHARLES C. CONVERSE

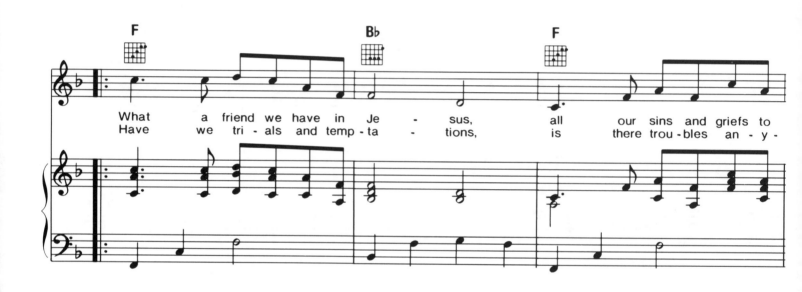

3. Are we weak and heavy laden,
   cumbered with a load of care?
   Precious Savior still our refuge;
   take it to the Lord in prayer.
   Do thy friends despise, forsake thee?
   Take it to the Lord in prayer.
   In His arms He'll take and shield thee;
   thou will find a solace there.

WHEN I SURVEY
THE WONDROUS CROSS

Words by ISAAC WATTS
Music by LOWELL MASON

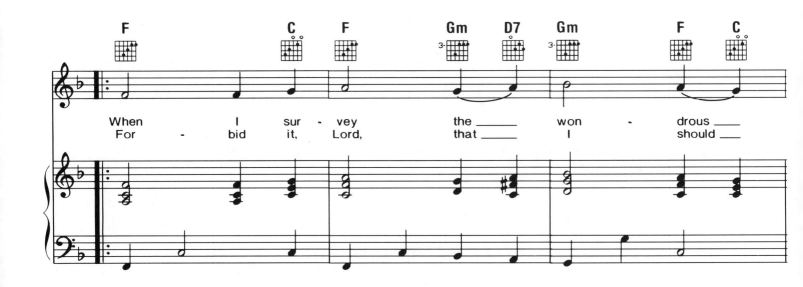

When I sur - vey the won - drous
For - bid it, Lord, that I should

cross On which the Prince of
boast Save in the death of

3. See, from His head, His hands, His feet,
Sorrow and love flow mingled down
Did e'er such love and sorrow meet
Or thorns compose so rich a crown.

4. Were the whole realm of nature mine,
That were a present far too small.
Love so amazing so divine,
Demands my soul, my life, my all.

WHITER THAN SNOW

Words by JAMES NICHOLSON
Music by WILLIAM G. FISCHER

1. Lord Je - sus, I long to be per - fect - ly whole; I
2.-4. *(See additional verses)*

want Thee for - ev - er to live in my soul, Break

down ev - ery i - dol, cast out ev - 'ry foe; Now

Additional Verses

2. Lord Jesus, look down from Thy throne in the skies,
   And help me to make a complete sacrifice;
   I give up myself, and whatever I know,
   Now wash me and I shall be whiter than snow.
   REFRAIN

3. Lord Jesus, for this I most humbly entreat,
   I wait, blessed Lord, at Thy crucified feet;
   By faith, for my cleansing I see Thy blood flow,
   Now wash me and I shall be whiter than snow.
   REFRAIN

4. Lord Jesus, Thou seeest I patiently wait,
   Come now, and within me a new heart create;
   To those who have sought Thee, Thou never saidst "No,"
   Now wash me and I shall be whiter than snow.
   REFRAIN

WONDERFUL WORDS OF LIFE

Words and Music by
PHILIP P. BLISS

WONDROUS LOVE

Southern American Folk Hymn

WHEN THE ROLL IS CALLED UP YONDER

Words and Music by
JAMES M. BLACK